PRAISE FOR
PSYCHICS, HEALERS, AND MEDIUMS

"Jenniffer's research into the lives of the intuitively gifted is both fascinating and often hilarious. A must read for the spiritually curious."

—Judith Orloff, MD, author of *Second Sight*

"Being a lifelong spiritual seeker and journalist lends credibility to Jenniffer's pursuit of Truth, and this book reflects that intention. As with any profession, there will be those who operate from integrity and those who do not. Jenniffer clearly sifts through that mix and offers an engaging, inspiring, and promising read! It will leave you with your own sense of authentic faith that there are, in fact, many gifted healers on this planet, and psychic phenomena are real."

—Rebecca Rosen, author of *Awaken the Spirit Within* and *Spirited*

"Jenniffer Weigel takes her readers on a rollicking adventure into the paranormal and its practitioners. A wise, funny, and incisive book written by a first-class interviewer."

—Paul Selig, author of *I Am the Word*

PSYCHICS,
HEALERS,
AND
MEDIUMS

OTHER BOOKS BY
JENNIFFER WEIGEL

This Isn't the Life I Ordered

Stay Tuned

I'm Spiritual, Dammit!

PSYCHICS, HEALERS, AND MEDIUMS

*A Journalist, a Road Trip,
and Voices from the Other Side*

Jenniffer Weigel

HAMPTON ROADS

Cover design by Jim Warner
Cover icons © Daria Rosen
Interior by Maureen Forys, Happenstance Type-O-Rama
Typeset in Adobe Garamond Pro and Gotham Pro

Hampton Roads Publishing Company, Inc.
Charlottesville, VA 22906
Distributed by Red Wheel/Weiser, LLC
www.redwheelweiser.com

Sign up for our newsletter and special offers by going to
www.redwheelweiser.com/newsletter/.

ISBN: 978-1-57174-776-1
Library of Congress Cataloging-in-Publication Data available upon
request

Printed in Canada
MAR
10 9 8 7 6 5 4 3 2 1

*To all who dare to question or
challenge the status quo.*

CONTENTS

PREFACE

FOR THE PAST COUPLE OF DECADES, I've interviewed many people who claim to have unusual talents. Some call themselves intuitive healers. Others profess to be mediums with the ability to talk to the dead. And then there are the psychics who want to tell me what happens next Tuesday. As a journalist, I'm naturally skeptical of anything that can't be proven through traditional sources; someone you can see, hear, touch, or call on the phone. Still, I've had many encounters through my interviews that have left me scratching my head. This curiosity keeps me up at night and inspires me to dig deeper into my research as I continue my quest for clarity.

My journey into the world of mediums, psychics, and healers is a personal one. I lost my dad to brain cancer in 2001 and quickly realized that grief is a very pricey business. I felt it was my duty to investigate those offering grief support in the metaphysical world and pass on the information to others who are struggling with a loss so they could avoid wasting their time and money.

Some colleagues think I've lost my mind for even venturing into these conversations. I like to remind them that smoking used to be a universally acceptable practice (complete with doctors appearing in commercials lighting up Camels). Today, we have ads saying secondhand smoke causes cancer in our cats. Our version of "truth" is based on the information that has been collected up until that point. We continue to evolve as we gather more evidence.

I think there is a spiritual evolution happening as well—a kind of collective consciousness or inquisitive spirit that is percolating in living rooms, businesses, and schools all over the world. I'm meeting people who are questioning everything they've known to be true on a regular basis, either because they've experienced something they can't explain or they have an intuition they can no longer suppress.

Even before my father got sick, I'd been curious about intuition. As a young child, I remember having a sense of "knowing" about events before they would happen. I would get a "gut feeling" around certain people who had ill intentions. Eventually my mom took me to the pediatrician who said I was "just making up stories for attention." I decided it was best to shut down whatever intuition I had at the time and tried to fit in.

Years later in the mid-1990s, when I was just out of college, I had an intriguing encounter with a psychic named Denise Guzzardo. She was a friend of a friend who lived in a farmhouse an hour and a half outside Chicago. In an era before Google, she managed to tell me things about my career and relationship at the time that nobody outside my immediate circle could have known. I racked my brain for weeks trying to figure out how she could have gathered the information ahead of time.

When I was working for CBS, I shared my paranormal interests with a colleague who admitted that he, too, was curious about mediums and psychics. While on location for an assignment in London, he'd heard about a medium doing an event around the corner from our hotel. We had some time to kill before our interviews and decided to go see what it was all about. When we mentioned to the locals we were "going to see a medium," nobody seemed phased. It was as normal to them as if we had said we were going to the movies. I soon realized that the stigma attached to mediums and psychics was much more common in the United States than it is in Europe.

The "event" was a tiny room with about fifty chairs facing a platform on a very intimate stage. The medium stood in front of the crowd keeping her hands cupped together as she addressed the audience. She had white hair, a Scottish accent, and a sweet disposition. I don't even remember her name—she wasn't selling any books and didn't seem to be well-known outside of her small community. She was very specific with every message she delivered. There was nothing vague like, "I see a man and he's sending love." She would say, "I have Sue Ellen here. She loves the blue shoes you wore at the funeral." I was amazed at her details and kept looking for wires, wondering if she had a little microphone in her ear giving her information.

She had one statement that she repeated often as she nodded to the air in gratitude for the messages that came through:

"I know what you're sayin' that way!"

Although with her thick Scottish brogue it sounded more like,

"I kneeew what yer sayin' dat weeeeehhhhh!"

The most emotional message she gave that day was for one couple who had lost their young daughter. She described what the daughter was wearing the day she died and even gave details about the shape and color of the stained-glass window where the father prayed to his daughter every morning. After the messages were delivered, a huge weight seemed to lift off both their shoulders like an anchor when it comes out of the water. I followed the couple out of the hall when the session was over and watched their interactions to see if perhaps they could have been planted in the audience. Judging by the way they held each other for dear life as they wept on the sidewalk, I knew right away that they were just two parents looking for a sign that their beloved daughter was safe and out of pain.

This book is a collection of evidence and encounters with well-known authors in this spiritual space. The subjects range from mediums ("I see dead people") to psychics ("I predict your future") to medical intuitives ("I can look at you and see why you are ill"). Some of them cross many platforms with multiple abilities while others focus on one specific gift. All of them believe their gifts to be very real.

"The Manhattan Medium" Thomas John says, "Intuition is like singing in the shower. Some people are really good at it and other people are not so good, but everyone can do it." So we all have intuitive abilities. For some of us, it comes easier than for others.

And for those who choose to shut down their intuition or believe reaching out to mediums goes against the Bible, I'd like to share this email sent to me by a Roman Catholic priest after I told him I get a lot of flack from religious people who feel I'm going to hell for doing this research:

"The Bible is full of references to mediums. 1 Sam 28 acknowledges the existence of mediums in Israel, and while Saul had forbidden the practice, he himself went to a medium to call up the spirit of Samuel, and Samuel is annoyed that he has been called back. But he did come and speak to Saul through the medium. I also think the Resurrection of Jesus confirms this further stage of existence. When Jesus appears to Mary Magdalene, he tells her not to touch him because he has not yet ascended to the Father. There is plenty in the scriptures to assure you and anyone willing to listen that you are not a kook for exploring this and that you are in touch with something very real."

I'm not trying to force my beliefs onto anyone else. I'm just sharing exactly what happened to me with each encounter so people can draw their own conclusions.

While some names have been changed to protect the identity of those who wish not to be recognized, everything in this book is true. So as you read the chapters, and perhaps come across stories that might seem too strange for your current belief system to embrace, remember this: The dropping of nuclear bombs was a spectator sport in the deserts of Nevada back in the 1950s. We do what we think is best based on the knowledge we have at the time. Asking questions and gathering information is the only way to expand our consciousness.

And you just can't make this shit up.

Jenniffer Weigel

1

Thomas John, "The Manhattan Medium"

THOMAS JOHN, AKA "THE MANHATTAN MEDIUM," first started talking to dead people at the tender age of four. His grandpa Leo, who had died five years before Thomas was born, often came to visit him at night with specific messages for Thomas to deliver to his parents. One message in particular that truly rattled the family was when Thomas revealed that his grandpa's watch, which had gone missing after Leo died, had been taken by a close family friend. When this was proven to be true, Thomas's parents were still unwilling to accept that he was talking to ghosts. They took him to every therapist, priest, and rabbi they could get their hands on to help their son cope with his "issues."

When Thomas was ten, his family met a Roman Catholic priest who actually encouraged them to let Thomas talk to the other side, saying that the Bible was indeed written by "mystics" and "seers" and that Thomas had "angels" talking to him. This helped ease some tensions, but Thomas still had a very chaotic childhood. His father was verbally and physically abusive, and Thomas did his best to keep the peace for himself and his younger sisters, often leaning on his maternal grandmother for comfort.

The spirits continued to show up in Thomas's life, yet he didn't plan to make a career out of seeing dead people until after he graduated from the University of Chicago with a degree in psychology. He eventually *came out* to his family, both about being gay and being a medium, and while some of his religious family members still mail him Bibles in the hopes of helping him to avoid "burning in hell," he now has clients all over the world, including celebrities such as Courteney Cox and Jenny McCarthy.

My first encounter with Thomas came on a hot day in June in 2015. I was scheduled to interview him for my monthly author series at the Wilmette Theatre on his book *Never Argue with a Dead Person: True and Unbelievable Stories from the Other Side*, which was just being released. We decided to meet in the lobby of his Chicago hotel where he would give me a reading during my lunch hour on the day of our event.

I had been working as a columnist at the *Chicago Tribune* for five years and had just been given notice a few days prior that my services were no longer needed. Having thought I was actually up for a promotion and not in danger of losing my job, I was completely blindsided. I had to keep coming to work for three more weeks and was told that no announcement would be made about my leaving until my last day. They also insisted that I keep the news quiet to avoid any negative press.

I decided not to share the truth with anyone (except my boyfriend at the time) until the end of the month—not even my family. Meanwhile, I had coincidentally just put my house on the market and was dealing with a very high-maintenance buyer who was struggling to grasp the meaning of the term "as-is."

"They want a fifteen thousand dollar credit for a new roof and updated electric," my real estate attorney told me on the phone before I was about to walk into my meeting with Thomas.

"What part of AS-IS do they not understand?!" I yelled. "Kill the deal."

There was silence on the other end of the phone. While my lawyer was also annoyed that our buyers were a pain in the ass, I don't think he expected me to pull the plug.

"It was our first offer," I said. "We will get another one."

"Okay, I will let the buyer's attorney know," he said.

I hung up the phone, took a deep breath, and went inside the hotel.

Damn!

As Thomas approached, I was struck by his height. He was tall, dark, and handsome, and wore blue jeans and a dark jean jacket. His demeanor was quiet, and his voice was soft and pitched higher than I expected.

"Let's sit over here," he said, choosing a spot in the lobby with privacy. "So have you done something like this before?"

"Oh, yes," I said. "I have written three books about people like you."

Having interviewed dozens of mediums and psychics since my father died of a brain tumor in 2001, I've experienced everything from total frauds to people who knew stuff they couldn't possibly have known ahead of time and everything in between. If Thomas wanted to scam me, he could find a slew of facts online very easily. I was looking for the things you can't research—the stuff that only *I* would know.

Like the fact that I'd just killed a real estate deal before walking through the door!

"So let me focus here, and we will see what comes up," he said, twisting his silver ring on his finger while he closed his eyes.

"I know it's a common name but do you have a John who has died?"

"Yes, I do," I said. "My grandfather."

"I sort of felt a not nice energy from him, like kinda mean and tough," he said.

My Grandpa John thrived on conflict and was known for not speaking to family members for years if they didn't agree with his way of thinking. He had four marriages and didn't bother to learn some of his grandchildren's names. "Kinda mean and tough" was right on target.

"He seems like he was a little narcissistic, like he just cared about himself," he said. "This is on your dad's side. So this must be your dad's dad."

"Indeed," I said.

"I'm not sure what he's doing here," he said with a laugh. "It's like he wants to make this about him."

Sounds like John.

"I don't want to freak you out, so I don't know if this is actually something very recent or something coming up, but your dad is stepping through—your dad is making me aware of some sort of job shift," he said. "It's either just about to happen or it just happened."

Holy shit!

"Yes," I whispered.

"I feel like this is a wide-open thing for you," he said. "By the way, is anyone in St. Louis?"

"Yes, my brother just moved there," I said.

"Your dad is bringing that up," he said. "And someone else is moving there, too. You don't know about it yet, but it's in the works. It will be a surprise."

Really?

"Who is the little Aries around you?" he asked. "Feels like a boy."

"My son Britt's birthday is April 14," I said. "Is that Aries?"

"Yeah, that's Aries," he said. "Your dad didn't meet him, but he definitely knows about him. Now with your son, is he changing schools?"

Within the last twenty-four hours, Britt's father and I had been discussing the fact that we were not happy with our son's school and wanted to make a switch.

"We were *just* thinking about it," I said. "He's going into fourth grade."

5

"I'm feeling like you want to look into it," he said. "It's not for the academic but more for the social, emotional piece. His school now is not 100 percent of a social fit. He seems very sensitive to me—very hyperaware. I do see a good trajectory with him, though."

Good to know.

"With the work stuff, your dad is stepping in here," he said. "This seems like something he wants to help you with. I don't know if he was someone you would go to for advice on job stuff, but he is sort of taking that over."

My father had been a journalist for thirty years. When he was alive, we talked every day, mostly about work.

"He's saying you are better off," he said. "It's actually a good thing because I don't feel a good energy with that company. It's negative. You're better off being away from it."

Anyone who worked inside the *Tribune* at the time called it the "Toxic Tower."

"Your dad is saying the summer will be kind of light and getting some of your own projects started," he said. "Something will present itself in September. Basically until then there will be money to float. Your dad is showing me Washington, DC. Does somebody connect there?"

"My sister goes to college there," I said.

"Your dad is bringing her up, too," he said. "He's happy you two are close, even though there's an age difference. But they keep showing me September. Somewhere in September there is a big work opportunity that gets presented to you. They're showing me a circle. It's almost like you're going full circle, like returning to your roots. In a positive way, not like you're spinning your wheels. Like you may have thought, 'I don't want to do that anymore, that's kind of my past life,' but opportunities might come up that bring you back to what you might have done before. That might be what I'm seeing in September."

Bring it on!

"You've done a lot of healing around your dad, and since his passing, you've been on quite a journey," he said. "He's very proud of you and what you're doing. You're holding your own, and you're not giving up. You only have the son, right?"

"Yes," I said.

"There's a little girl that I see around you," he said. "I don't know who this is, but there's a little girl that I'm seeing who is going to be in your life. Someone you look to like a daughter. Are you single?"

"I'm dating someone," I said.

The guy I'd been seeing, let's call him Jason because that's totally *not* his name, is someone I'd been dating for about a year. While things had seemed to be going well, I noticed him pulling back on me when I told him the news about my job.

"Okay, he really likes you, but your dad is saying he has commitment issues," Thomas said. "One thing they're telling me is that you will know within this year if this relationship is going to happen. This isn't going to drag on for five years."

Thomas sat for a few seconds and started twisting his ring.

"There's another person coming through," he said. "Do you have a Martha anywhere?"

OMG!

"Martha was my sister-in-law," I said. "We were very close but haven't talked much since her brother and I got divorced."

"I feel someone is connecting with her," he said. "Your mother-in-law had cancer, right?"

"Yes," I said.

"This must be her," he said. "You must have been involved in her passing."

My dad died of cancer on Father's Day, 2001. My mother-in-law died two years later, on Father's Day as well. I was present when each of them took their last breath.

"I feel that even though you aren't married to her son anymore, you two still have a connection," he said. "I get a very pushy energy from her. She has a real presence to me. Kind of a smart-ass!"

Affirmative!

Kathy taught her sons how to throw a baseball and cared more about the Chicago Cubs than most men. She had a wicked sense of humor and chain-smoked skinny cigarettes. I missed her every day.

"And who is Richard?" he asked.

"That was my ex-father-in-law," I said.

"He's here, too," he said. "They are both very connected to your son."

While Thomas could have researched my Grandpa John's name and my brother moving to St. Louis or sister being in DC, it would have been nearly impossible to find out the name of my ex-sister-in-law Martha or former in-laws, Kathy and Richard.

And then, "I see you moving, too," he said. "Did you just pull out of a deal for like a house sale or something? Like TODAY?"

SHUT-THE-FRONT-DOOR!

"Yes," I said, totally amazed.

"I feel like that was a good thing to do," he said. "You don't want to do business with those people. Just pretend like it never even happened. I see you getting a much cleaner offer in about three weeks."

You can't Google THAT!

Later that evening, Thomas and I sat on the stage of the Wilmette Theatre in front of a sold-out audience of 150 people. I shared with the room my experience from earlier that day and how Thomas managed to mention things that had not been public knowledge, including the house deal that went bust.

Thomas then went on to explain that his information comes through clairvoyantly, or the gift of seeing, as well as clairaudiently (clear hearing).

"We're all really psychics and mediums in a way—we all have that ability," he said. "It's kind of like singing in the shower. Some people are really good at it and some people kind of suck at it. But everyone can do it."

Thomas was much more relaxed and really showed his sense of humor on the stage. I like to think it was because he was starting to feel more comfortable around me, but it probably had more to do with the Pinot Grigio we'd shared in the greenroom.

"This started for you when you were just four years old," I said. "How was that for your parents?"

"I grew up Catholic in a home where it was like, 'Don't do that, and don't talk about that,'" he said.

"So you grew up Catholic, and gay, and a medium," I said. "Talk about pushing a boulder up hill with your family! Do they like you now?"

"My mom is my biggest supporter," he said. "I am not close with my dad. When I was growing up, like twenty-five years ago, there weren't people on TV doing this. There wasn't a whole Barnes & Noble section on psychics and mediums, so my mom was scared. She said, 'We thought something was wrong with you, and we were scared of you. We literally thought there were demons inside of you.' They thought I had Asperger syndrome, maybe autism, that I was bipolar. I would come to her and say things that would happen the next day, and she and my dad were totally freaked out by it. And now they understand. That's just education. I have people calling me from all across the country saying, 'My five-year-old sees auras and is talking to my dead dad,' so with kids it's always a big deal trying to figure out what's going on."

"My son has seen my dead dad since he was two, and my dad died years before he was born," I said. "He doesn't talk about it at school because obviously that's weird, and kids want to play dodgeball and not talk to ghosts. Did you shut down your gift when you were a child?"

"Oh, sure," he said. "Because we haven't created anything in our culture and society that has a way to nurture that. And I think that goes to a larger issue—I mean we are the only species that kills our own children. We're not the best nurturers. We need to come up with a better system for dealing with these kinds of things and embracing children like that, because why should we have to shut it down? There needs to be a new dialogue. 'So you can talk to dead people, how does that help the world? What's the reason for that? Why would somebody who is dead come back and talk to you?' I think it's mostly about healing."

"For those who don't know the difference, mediums talk to the dead and psychics predict the future," I said. "Some do both and some don't, but you do both."

"Yes," he said.

"So what if you predict something for somebody and then it doesn't happen?" I asked. "With free will, we can change our trajectory at any time, so does that make things difficult for you and what you do?"

"I try to tell people what opportunities may be around them," he said. "So I had a reading today with a woman whose son tragically died of a drug overdose. He came through and I blurted out this name and the woman said, 'That's the name of a book I wanted to write, but it's sitting on my computer at home, but nobody knows about it.' And I said, 'I think they want you to do that, because they're bringing it up.' Does that mean they're going to hang up the phone and call HarperCollins? No, but it gave her validation. But there has to be an effort that is put forth. Things won't happen for people who sit in a room and don't do anything. But when spirit comes through, they will often talk

about opportunities for people. As for predictions, sometimes I can see things, but the timing might be off. "

"You told me my house will sell in three weeks," I said.
"The timing better not be off for that one!"

"I definitely see you selling your house," he said. "It
might be a matter of *when* but it's not a matter of *if.*"

"You said that you don't like clients to become too
dependent on you," I said.

"Some clients just want answers, yet they don't want to
change," he said. "I had a client come to me and she said, 'I
want to know when I'm going to lose some weight,' and I
asked what her diet was like and she's talking about hoagies
and ice cream, which is great but you don't need a psychic
to tell you you're not going to lose weight if you keep eating
that stuff! But the guidance over the last two years has been
at a deeper level. For example I had a reading with this guy
this morning who asked, 'When am I going to find somebody?' He wanted to start dating someone. And what came
up was that he had this horrible trauma around his father's
death, and he said, 'Yeah, he died when I was twelve and I
have a lot of guilt because I found him on the floor and I
wasn't close to him.' So what they wanted for him was to
heal that trauma and work on that issue first before jumping
into a relationship. So they wouldn't just say, 'Go to the bar
and meet somebody!' You know? It's about giving people
more tools.

"And then there are other times. Like I have a friend who
called me and she said, 'I'm turning forty soon and I hate
to ask you, but do you see me getting married or having

kids?' And I don't know why this came to me, but I said, 'I think you need to go down to the bar that's beneath your building and I want you to go there for a couple nights. You're going to meet someone from your past.' The next day she was there and she met this guy she went to college with. They started talking, traded numbers, and they've been together ever since. So I know spirit was telling me, or her dead grandmother was telling me, that's what she needed to do. And sometimes it is that easy."

"How do you explain yourself to people who are completely convinced that you are Googling them ahead of time and think you're full of shit?" I asked.

"I have a lot to say about that," he said. "I think it's good to be skeptical. You should be cautious when dealing with people who are mediums and psychics because there are varying degrees of abilities. At the end of the day, you have to make your own judgment on this stuff. I've had people who have had really great readings, and it doesn't really help them for some reason. It's just not their thing. So I don't push it on people. People seek me out. If someone gives you an hour reading, there may be some things that would be on somebody's obituary, but there are always things that come up that you can't research that validate the connection.

"Obviously, there are charlatan psychics who say things that aren't true or they guess things or try to scare you, and most educated people will know those people are out there. But I think the ones that do more harm are the ones who are really trying to help people, but they haven't developed their ability enough or not gotten the proper training and haven't fleshed it out enough to be billing themselves that they are an intuitive or a healer. Then there are other people who have an ability but their ego or drive to be famous gets in the way, so they're more focused on that when it's supposed to be about the work."

"What do you think happens when we die?" I asked.

"Well, God rest her soul, but Sylvia Browne used to write these things about the other side, like 'There's fourteen white castles and then there's eighteen Angels with gold harps,' and it's like, 'How do you know?'" he said with a laugh. "What I do know is they stay connected to us. I know that for a fact. I do know that they still communicate with us. I do know that they know about things that happen after they die. I do know that they are aware of things that happen when perhaps they're not in a conscious state. They're not in pain anymore. They're not in a body anymore. Those are things that I can say are truths after reading so many people."

"Do you believe in reincarnation?" I asked.

"Yes, you can come back, but that has to be something that you want to do," he said. "You also have to have a reason. The interesting thing about the physical world is a lot of times it's our test. This is our school. Somebody that has a problem with drugs and alcohol—addiction doesn't exist on the other side. So somebody may want to come into the physical world and say 'I want to be free of that, so I'm going to test myself in the physical world because I was an addict in a past life and in this life I want to show that I can overcome that. And I'm going to be a spiritual teacher at the

Betty Ford Center.' They tell me there is a life review when you die and you see how you affected people. I also haven't been shown a hell or a devil with a pitchfork either. I think if there was a hell, they would have told me by now."

"What do you think of the Long Island Medium and the Hollywood Medium and all these mediums with TV shows?" I asked.

"I think when you're doing stuff with TV it's a slippery slope real quick," he said. "I've done lots of TV shows and appearances, and it has positives. The main positive is that it brings awareness of the gift to people that wouldn't normally seek it out on their own. But on TV, there is so much editing, trying to make it great TV, that it really makes it an entirely different energy form. It becomes an entirely different animal. It's not about the work anymore. I'd be more interested in a show that studies the science behind mediumship or performs studies about it that show it as a form of healing for people. Does this help people in grief? If someone wants to give Caitlyn Jenner a reading about what dress she's going to wear next week, great. But I really don't see the big value of it."

"How do you explain what you do to the religious folks who think it's the devil?"

"Well first off the Bible was written by psychics and prophets and mediums, and Jesus came back from the dead, which was a mediumistic experience," he said. "The Wise Men were following stars, so they were astrologers. What I've taken away from the Bible from being raised Catholic is never put seeing psychics and seers before God, because back then they would consult these people and put that before God. And I totally agree with that. Your connection to God is more important than anything else. Then come the other things. And that's why it kills me that people will come for a reading, and they don't believe in God or an afterlife or heaven, but they say, 'Am I going to meet anybody soon?' And I'll say, 'So we're going to call on the angels and spirit and your dead grandmother, but you don't believe in any of this?!' And they're like, 'Yeah, and when am I getting a raise?'"

After a few more questions, Thomas did readings for the crowd for nearly an hour. He brought up specific names over and over again, pulling out facts such as the color of a favorite football jersey to the decor of a dead child's bedroom. There were dogs and dads and grandparents and tattoo descriptions causing the audience to gasp more times than I could count.

"We should do this again!" I said to Thomas as we were signing books in the lobby.

"Yes we should!" he said.

✢ ✢ ✢

A few days later, we got a date on the calendar to have Thomas back to the Wilmette Theatre for another show in August. I posted it on Facebook, and within minutes, I was being flooded with messages telling me that Thomas was a fraud.

What are they talking about?

Apparently, a story had been written by the *New York Daily News* claiming Thomas was a scam artist and former drag queen named Lady Vera Parker. The online article claimed he had scammed someone out of money for a security deposit on Craigslist several years prior and that he did research on his subjects through PayPal before his readings, challenging his integrity. The tone of the article was very unprofessional and catty, but it still made me wonder. While I didn't care about his days as Lady Vera Parker (he actually looked quite beautiful in the photos), the Craigslist thing was a cause for concern. I didn't want to put my professional reputation in jeopardy.

"We need to talk," I texted Thomas.

Within minutes, we were on the phone.

"So I know we all have things in our past we aren't exactly proud of," I said, recalling an incident in high school that involved a fender bender and Coors Light. "Is this article true?"

"I tried to get out of a lease by subleasing it myself through Craigslist. It didn't go very well," he said. "I bounced a check and made a couple of bad choices. That was almost ten years ago, and that's not who I am anymore."

Thomas said that after the Craigslist mishap, he went home to the East Coast and got his life together. He said his gifts became much more pronounced when he decided it was time to start using them to help people.

"I've paid everybody back," he said. "We all make mistakes, and I am no exception."

"I'm actually relieved to know you're human," I said. "And people forgive when they're ready. I mean look at Bill Clinton! I think the best thing to do is come clean about this in our next show, because like you said, it's not who you are *now*. It was a blip in the radar screen of your past."

"Sounds good," he said.

Meanwhile, some of my friends were still not convinced, as if that article gave everyone free rein to think the worst. One guy thought Thomas had a transmitter in his ear giving him information during the show. Others were sure he got the list from the theater of those in attendance ahead of time and researched every tragic death on the North Shore before the event. Several emails came in, sending the link to that story in the *New York Daily News* with reasons why I should not do any more shows with the guy (or gal, depending on his outfit). I was exhausted trying to defend Thomas and my professional integrity to the city of Chicago.

A few days later, my mother tells me that she is moving to St. Louis.

Say what?!

"Thomas John mentioned that someone else was going to be moving to St. Louis in my reading," I said to her when she gave me the news.

But when three weeks after my Thomas reading came and went and I had no offer on my house, I was starting to feel discouraged.

"Hey, not even Michael Jordan made every basket," my friend reminded me. "The guy can't get *everything* right."

The August show soon approached and once again, it was sold out. We brought in the question about his past right at the start, and his readings for the crowd were even more impressive than they had been for the June show. The demand was so high for him to return that we immediately planned another date for the fall.

When September rolled around, I was offered a job hosting and producing a holiday-themed show for WCIU TV station in Chicago, which had been founded by my grandfather John Weigel (the crabby guy) in 1963. Thomas had mentioned that not only would I be getting a job in September, but also that something would be coming "full circle" and "returning to your roots." Grandpa John left WCIU in the '60s after a dispute with his partners. I was the first Weigel to be hired back at WCIU since 1964. That seemed pretty "full circle" and "returning to your roots" to me.

So that's why Grandpa was showing up in that reading . . .

As for my house sale, I'd finally gotten an offer from a really great buyer (four months later than I'd hoped, but better late than never).

The holidays came and went without much fanfare. And then, on a cold day in January, my boyfriend Jason came over for what I thought would be a night of cuddling in front of the football game. To my surprise, he broke up with me before I even had time to get out the chips and dip.

"I'm just not feeling it," he said.

Wow.

A few weeks went by, and I decided that working my ass off was the best medicine to nurse my breakup. I continued to do live events and podcasts with different authors, and in my research, I found out the story about Thomas in the *New York Daily News* had actually been planted by another male medium who was jealous of Thomas's rising fame and talent.

Aren't there enough dead people to go around for everyone?

At the same time, medical intuitive and best-selling author Caroline Myss, whom I introduced to Thomas after one of his shows, not only believed in his gifts, she decided to endorse his work publicly.

Talk about yin and yang.

One afternoon, I received a message on Facebook from a woman who had had a powerful reading from Thomas just days before, but was doubting the validity because of that article in the *New York Daily News*.

I'm so sick of this!

"What would you say to filming one of your spirit circles with people you don't know?" I asked Thomas, trying to come up with a way to establish proof. "That way, nobody could doubt the results, whatever they may be."

Thomas often hosted "spirit circles" with ten to twelve people, which is a more intimate way to connect with your loved ones who have passed. Within a smaller group, each person is guaranteed a connection. Since there was a waiting list to get into the circles, we decided to add one on the calendar for just six people. Three would be chosen from the waiting list on his website, and the others I would choose and keep all information about them to myself ahead of time. We would hold the event in my living room.

The three people I chose were my friend Joe, whose wife Molly had died tragically when a tree struck her while they were riding bikes in a forest preserve; Hal, whose partner Rik had passed away suddenly in his sleep; and Kim, whose son had died after suffering injuries in a car accident.

A couple weeks before the circle, Joe texted that he had a conflict and couldn't make it, so he would send Molly's best friend Michelle in his place.

On the day of the circle, Thomas didn't even know the sexes of the three people I had picked, let alone their names or who their dead people might be. We had a camerawoman rolling, and I pulled out my iPhone to record some backup audio.

As soon as Thomas began, Hal's partner came barreling through.

"Who is Rik?" he asked.

"That's my partner," Hal said.

"He's tall and showing me a mustache," he said. Hal nodded. "There is someone who keeps coming through with him, too; I'm getting somebody with some sort of military outfit. They might have done service and they were younger, and they would have passed from a suicide. Do you understand?"

"That was Rik's son," Hal said.

"He's definitely reconnected with him," Thomas said. "And he's very happy that he is remembered at the church, so I don't know if there's a special church he would go to, but he's bringing that up."

Rik had been a pastor for a spiritualist church in Chicago called "The Church of the Spirit." He was also a third-generation medium.

"I feel a very strong connection with him to spiritual stuff," Thomas said. "Paranormal, things like this. I feel like he would be open to hearing about it. I'm also supposed to acknowledge—do you understand the name Annie?"

"That's our granddaughter," Hal said with tears in his eyes.

"Even though he's not here anymore, he wants there to be a connection with you and her," Thomas said. "Was Rik a medium?" Hal nods. "It's funny because he keeps correcting my form. He said, 'Don't be lazy. Say what you're getting, you're really good!'"

"That's him!" Hal said.

Thomas went on to mention Rik's father "Deacon Dick" and Rik's son Rock. The connections were astounding. And then:

"Who is Molly? Because I have someone's very close friend coming through," Thomas said.

"That was my friend," Michelle said quietly.

"She's telling me that she passed very suddenly," he said. "She never saw this coming. Now, was there a head injury? In the back of the head?"

"Yes," Michelle said.

"She keeps showing me the letter J," he said. "Who is the J connection? She keeps showing me a J."

"Her husband," Michelle said.

"I feel she worries about him a lot," Thomas said. "I feel like you're sort of the next in command and she really trusts you to maybe tell him these things. She's saying also that this is a man that I see was very healthy and now maybe is not so much, so I feel like maybe diet and exercise—she's saying he needs to make sure that he's taking care of himself. This is such a tragedy, and he's really lost without her. I feel like the way she is acknowledging it is that she wants him to take care of himself and make sure that he's staying connected."

Joe's active lifestyle had fallen by the wayside when Molly died. Friends visited around the clock to check on him and spend time with him to help him through the loss, but doing daily cardio wasn't really on top on his "to-do" list.

"She also keeps showing me—I'm seeing like a Japanese or a Chinese sort of letter," Thomas said. "I don't know those languages, but I keep seeing this letter."

Michelle confirmed that Molly had a tattoo like the letter Thomas was seeing.

"This is more for this J person," he continued. "She wants him to be able to have love again. I feel like they had a very connected relationship, and she's telling me that she loved him very much. But since she's not in the physical world anymore, she wants him to be able to continue and still have that and be able to be intimate with somebody. I also feel like she's going to bring the person into his life in a way. Was she very funny?" Michelle nods. "I feel sort of like a dark sense of humor sometimes. It's almost like she's saying, 'What a fucked-up way to die? I can't believe I went that way!' I want you to know, I actually don't feel that her physical body was in a lot of pain. It was like her soul left kind of instantly. I don't feel like she was suffering. I feel like if you were there you would be like 'Oh, My God!' but I feel like the actual experience was not painful. It's almost like it happened so quickly that pain didn't register for her. She just wants people to know that. And I feel like her husband, he goes back there a lot—not back there physically but I feel like he rehashes that—and she's like, 'I don't want to be remembered like, dead on the ground with my head beat in. I want to be remembered for how I was in life.'"

Thomas then went on to read the others with the same clarity and specificity. Kim's son also came through, talking about everything from his nickname and how cool it is that he can eat junk food in heaven to how she was "the greatest mom."

After Thomas left, Kim, Michelle, and Hal stuck around to debrief about their experiences.

"Promise me you didn't tell him anything," Michelle said, clutching my arm.

"I didn't tell him one thing about any of you," I said, pointing to the three of them.

"Everything he said to me could have been found on Google," Kim said.

I couldn't believe my ears.

"He didn't know your name!" I said. "What was he going to Google? 'Siri, show me Jen's friends who might have a dead son, friend, or husband.' You can't Google when you don't have a starting point. He had no starting point!"

A few weeks later, I was having dinner with Thomas John and Caroline Myss, and I shared with Caroline the story of our "blind circle experiment."

"I've interviewed people who have drowned and come back to life, or survived twenty-five cancerous tumors. Those are living miracles. So why can people embrace those stories, and not this?" I asked. "I would get it if Thomas had been vague, but what he gave these people was so completely specific—stuff he couldn't know even with the best research team on the planet."

"I see this happen all the time with healing workshops," she said. "They have a healing and the faith in their own healing is not strong enough to sustain the impact of other peoples' doubts. I see it all the time. As a result they begin to doubt what they experienced themselves. And therefore their illness returns because what happens is the skepticism of others becomes the stronger psychic field."

The skepticism of others becomes the stronger psychic field.

"I am convinced this is why so many people do not heal at a speed faster than the collective mind," she continued. "Because they can't bring themselves to experience things outside the speed of what they are used to. So with an instantaneous healing, which would be faster than the ordinary speed, their sense of self is not strong enough to sustain that healing against the skepticism. So they go from believing to 'I must be a fool. I guess you're right.' Those doubting thoughts are all it takes."

"For every one of those skeptics, we get like fifty really great emails, though," Thomas said with a smile, sipping his wine.

The next day, Wendy Sharon, the executive director of the Wilmette Theatre, forwarded me one of those "really great" emails.

Hi Wendy,

I was at your show recently with Thomas John. My son came through to Thomas who committed suicide. I want to tell Mr. John how much that reading helped me. I also said "no" to a few things that really were correct, I just completely forgot.

I must say, I was raised by born-again Christians, and we learned that this was against God. But I have been searching. I saw it on your website, and purchased a ticket the day before. I was so freaked out, I even used a fake name so he would have no idea who I am. Everything Thomas said was so spot-on. What's even more, I played it for my husband, and he also now believes.

Thank you for being open to hosting an event like this. It completely changed our lives. We are so thankful.

Please let Thomas and Jen know we reached out.

Julie and Dan
Wilmette IL

2

Echo Bodine

I FIRST HEARD ABOUT ECHO BODINE from my publisher.

"She's a hoot," he said. "You will love her. Her whole family is psychic."

The whole family?

Raised Baptist in Minneapolis, Echo's life changed at the age of seventeen when her brother saw a ghost walk through the wall while he was playing the drums in the family room. Her mother Mae called on a local medium to get answers, who told her all of her children had intuitive gifts. Echo started studying the paranormal to see if she could develop her skills and discovered she was gifted with several of the "clairs": clairvoyance (the gift of seeing), clairaudience (hearing), clairsentience (sensing), and clairolfactance (smell). She's been a psychic, healer, and ghost buster since 1979 and has written several books including *What Happens When We Die: A Psychic's Exploration of Death, Heaven, and the Soul's Journey After Death* and *Echoes of the Soul: The Soul's Journey Beyond the Light—Through Life, Death, and Life after Death.*

Her younger brother Michael is a psychic who does ghost busting with his son Blake, and her sister Nikki is a practicing medium. They all live in the Minneapolis area.

I called Echo and scheduled a date to drive to Minneapolis so we could meet and I could observe one of her Intuitive Development classes. Even over the phone, I could tell she was hilarious.

"This is going to be fun, honey!" she said, as if we'd known each other for decades.

Echo told me she prefers to do her readings over the phone because often the energy of a client can interfere with her "signal." My initial reaction to this method allowed my inner skeptic to creep in.

Is that so you can have your computer open in front of you as you Google your subjects?

She also agreed to read a friend of my choosing. All I told Echo was that her first name was "Marie." (While she could Google the shit out of me, there was no way she could do any research on Marie.)

As the days approached for my phone reading, I was getting very excited to hear what she would have to say. She'd written a gaggle of books, had the respect of her peers, and has been doing this work for fifty years.

Meanwhile, I'd been struggling emotionally over the breakup with Jason. While it had been a couple months since he had left me crying on my couch in my best lingerie, he'd gone completely radio silent. I was curious to see what Echo would pick up.

Our scheduled phone appointment was for a Wednesday, but a few days prior, I got an email from Echo that she was feeling "extremely in tune" and was wondering if we could talk that day. I arranged a playdate for my son, got my questions ready (I was allowed up to five), and gave her a call.

"So, honey, the way this works is you tell me the questions you'd like to ask, and then what I do is I set the phone down for about a minute. And I light some sweetgrass, and then I say a little prayer, and I ask God to be as clear and accurate as possible," she said.

My questions were very basic and had to do with what work opportunities might come up and whether or not I'd find someone better than Jason.

"Once the pictures start to come, I pick up the phone. I work with an angel named Lilli, and so if you hear me say, 'She says this, she says that,' that's Lilli. Okay, sweetie? Just give me a minute and I'll be right back."

I sat on my bed and took a few deep breaths.

How many mountains do I have to climb to be assigned an angel like Lilli!?

Within a minute, she was back.

"Here we go. There's a lot of energy in the area of work, and I'm getting the number two, which I think is two months," she said. "There's something coming that is more solid, but you don't know about it yet. She shows me a picture of you with sunglasses on, which means you're not seeing the area of your career clearly. It's dark right now. The glasses stay on for a while. It's like you're walking around not knowing where to go: 'Should I walk around? Sit still? Get proactive and make something happen?'"

That sounds like me.

"I see someone coming along and putting you in a chair and saying, 'Just sit there and be quiet.' The chair they put you in is a high chair. It's like if the Universe could duct tape you to a chair, they would. Then someone puts the sun-glasses on you, and it's like, 'Now sit there, shut up, and stop trying to figure this all out!' And you're like, 'I NEED some guidance. You've got to help me.' I see the number two so in two months—you hear about something in May," she said.

May works for me, thanks.

"Then I see you in June, and I get an image of fire-crackers going off, you singing 'Alleluia,' and it feels like it comes out of left field. You are a very gifted writer and the Universe needs you. So you're never going to be without money," she said.

Sweet!

"The issue is going to be the steadiness of it—to be guar-anteed a paycheck every two weeks. That's not always going to be the case."

Dammit!

"On the one hand, you would like to have that secure check, but you're not willing to pay a price for it. She says that God or the Universe respects that about you. You're not willing to sell yourself short for fear of not having enough money."

This was so accurate. I'd left my network news job several years ago because I couldn't stand the negativity.

"Everything's wrong in the world, now back to you in the studio."

"The Universe is always going to have your back," she said. "Holy smokes! If you could see these pictures, you'd be laughing at yourself for even wondering if it was going to work out. I have this image of five irons in the fire, and all of it feels like, I would say by this June, it looks really fun if you can be okay with this flow. Now let's jump over to your love life. Lilli shows me a picture of a man you were just in a relationship with, and she says, 'He was down about a quart.'"

Affirmative.

"Now she shows me a picture of a brick," Echo said. "Stubborn as a brick. He didn't want the drama. He didn't want to have to explain much. It's just like, 'Okay, this is over now. Gotta go.' She's showing me a picture of weights. If you had stayed with him, he would have been a weight around your neck. You were like the turtle and the hare: him being the turtle and you being the hare running circles around him."

Interestingly, every time I explained my relationship with Jason to friends, I would use the tortoise and the hare analogy to show that we were just going at different speeds. While anyone can guess that I had a boyfriend, it's simply not possible to research a dynamic. She picked up on his attitude and his tempo. That stuff *can't* be Googled. And she—with the help of Lilli—nailed it.

"What I see is that you need to make these five connections, these five irons in the fire. You need to get these five things established before you meet the person that's going to be really significant to you. I just saw a picture of you laughing because you meet a guy," she continued.

Hooray!

"I see you giggling because you're on the phone with a friend saying, 'You're not going to believe this! Isn't that a strange place to meet somebody?' The person looks tall. You're not even looking for someone. It's just so goofy. It's easy. It's fun. It's out of the blue. It will be strange the way the two of you meet, and it will give you quite a giggle. But for right now, just remember you need to focus on the five irons in the fire. It's an important healing time for your heart, too. She says your heart is not actually broken, but it's got a few scars on it and you need to heal it, honey."

"Is there any timing as to when I'll meet this tall man in a mysterious place?" I asked.

"She said that it feels nearby—this year for sure. Can't tell you the exact timing because of the five irons in the fire. Feels like summertime. There's such a good image of you healed. You're ready for life. Things will happen fast and quick, and it will be a fun, crazy summer. Yikes! Change happens. You know what's so obvious to me in all these pictures she's showing me is that your life is just so well planned out."

You mean this was all part of a plan??!!

A few days later, Marie and I headed to Minneapolis.

"I'm really excited, but I'm kind of nervous, too," she said as she got in my Subaru to make our six-and-a-half-hour drive. "I'll order us a hotel room online while we're on the road."

Marie is a single mother of four who lost her son Joe tragically in a car accident when he was just twenty-two. He and some friends had been drinking all night and then decided to drive. They eventually crashed into a tree. Joe, who was in the passenger's seat, was the only casualty.

"It was a disaster waiting to happen," she said.

Joe was social, successful, and the guy everybody loved.

"Nineteen hundred people attended his funeral," she said. "There are probably 100 people who thought they were his best friend. That's how he made everybody feel. So many people came up to me and said, 'I am a better person because I knew your son,' from teachers to friends to coworkers. It was incredible."

As we made our way out of Illinois, the snow started to fall—hard.

"A blizzard in March?" I asked. "That's inconvenient."

Usually when I take long drives, I see hawks, either perched in the trees or soaring overhead. On this day, there were no hawks in sight, but a plethora of crows. I counted over twenty in the first two hours, which has never happened to me before.

Many of the gurus I've met have told me signs in nature can be winks from the other side. I interviewed Dr. Mary Neal, a best-selling author and orthopedic surgeon who had

had a near-death experience from a kayaking accident. In her book *To Heaven and Back*, she talks about the many miracles that have happened to her that can't be explained in simple terms. When you think "That's weird?! Must be a coincidence," those moments aren't coincidences at all, but actually God showing up in your life. I really took what she said to heart, because Dr. Neal is a woman of science who was without oxygen for thirty minutes. She is a living miracle.

"Can you look up the spiritual meaning of the crow?" I asked Marie, realizing this was an odd request.

"Uh, sure," she said, grabbing her phone.

After a few minutes, she had an answer.

"Many cultures consider crows to be the keepers of the Sacred Law, for nothing escapes their keen sight," she said, reading from her device. "The crow teaches us to have the wisdom to know ourselves beyond the limitations of one-dimensional thinking and laws. We are taught to appreciate the many dimensions of both reality and ourselves and to learn to trust our intuition and personal integrity."

"Wow!" I said.

"It can also represent the archetype of a trickster or jokester," she added. "They love a good prank."

"Prank, huh?" I said, wondering what "tricks" might be in store for us over the next twenty-four hours.

The snow continued to fall, and I did my best to concentrate on the road. I listened to Marie call several hotels as she tried to wheel and deal us a good rate.

"Is that the best you can do?" she asked. "That price won't work for us. What about free wi-fi? Can you get us free wi-fi? And maybe breakfast?"

After some fearless negotiating, Marie got us a room, free wi-fi, and free bottled water for only $109 for the night. I was so impressed with her tenacity.

I'd never be so bold!

The plan was to check in to the hotel and then Marie would get a phone reading. After their chat, we would meet Echo for dinner before both of us attended the Intuitive Development class.

"It's snowing sideways out there," I said, looking out at the blizzard when we arrived in our room.

By now, a few inches had stuck on the ground. We heard rumblings that over a foot had fallen in other areas.

Marie got her phone out along with her list of questions for Echo as I put my phone next to hers to record the session.

When Echo called, I could hear some tension in her voice.

"I may have to cancel tonight's class because of this snow," she said. "I'm also on the tail end of a migraine here, so I'm feeling a little out of sorts."

Oh, no! We came all this way!

"We can do this in person if that's better?" Marie offered.

"Let's give it a try this way, and we will see," Echo said. "Go ahead and give me your questions, and we will see what we get here."

Marie looked at me with wide eyes as she started to read her questions.

"I'd like to know, what is my life purpose for this life? What do you see in terms of a long-term romantic relationship in my future? I also have some overall questions about my job and career," she said.

"What do you do?" Echo asked.

"I work in learning and development for a big four accounting firm—internal training," she said.

That entire job description sounded like Swahili to me.

"Okay," Echo said.

"And I have several people on the other side including my son Joe, and I was wondering if anyone is strongly coming through?" Marie added.

"How old was Joe? And how long ago did he pass?" Echo asked.

"Twenty-two, and it was almost three years ago," Marie said.

"How old are you right now?" Echo asked.

"I'm fifty," Marie said.

"Okay, I think that's all I need. So what you need to do is you need to give me about a minute to do my ritual on my end, and as soon as my information starts to come, I will pick up the phone and come back," Echo said.

We sat and waited . . . and waited . . . and waited for what felt like forever.

And then:

"Okay, I'm not getting anything," Echo said.

We killed the psychic hotline!

"Hang in there with me. I don't know why it's taking so long," Echo said. "I'm going to hang up the phone. I don't know what's the matter, but sometimes it's just blank. When the weather is really goofy, this happens sometimes. Plus with the migraine, that could be part of it, too. So what I'm going to do is hang up the phone and try to sit here and try to relax. And then as soon as the information comes, I'll call you back."

Echo hung up the phone, and we sat there dumbfounded. I started to wonder if we were indeed being psychically pranked.

Was this what the crow was trying to warn us about?

"Now she can look me up since I gave her all that information," Marie said, putting on her skeptic hat.

"She doesn't have your last name," I said. "What's she going to do, try to find every fifty-year-old Marie who works in learning and development for a big four accounting firm from the Chicago area?!"

I felt bad for Echo. She had to deal with a snowstorm, a migraine, a reporter writing a book, and a stranger waiting to discover her "life purpose." I would not want to be in her shoes.

We watched the snow continue to fall from our hotel room. A few minutes later, Echo sent us an email that she had to cancel her class due to the weather and she suggested we meet at the restaurant called Huey's located next to the center where the class would have taken place. After eating, hopefully, Marie could get her reading.

Minutes later, we arrived at Huey's, which hardly looked like it would deliver anything decent, let alone something delicious as Echo insisted.

"Maybe I'm just unreadable?" Marie said in disappointment as we perused the menu.

Echo came in moments later wearing a fleece (complete with Nebraska logo) black leggings, and UGG boots. She had spiked blondish-gray hair, big beautiful blue eyes, and an infectious energy.

"Hey there!" she said, giving us both huge hugs. "Let's order something here, and then we can take it next door to eat."

"What's good?" I asked.

"Everything," she said. "They make it all fresh."

We put in our orders and got settled in a window table as we waited for the food.

"Is it okay if we chat a little now?" I asked, taking out my phone to record our conversation.

"Of course, sweetie," she said. "Anything you need."

"Has this ever happened when you try to tune in to someone and it's static?" Marie asked.

"Yes, sometimes when this happens, it's that the timing is off. I was trying to get my third eye open, and then I thought, 'Maybe this is because I'm supposed to do it in person?'—because I can do it in person but I don't normally. Let's see if it opens up after we eat," Echo said.

"Do you ever think this work depletes you physically?" I asked. "You talk a lot about doing healings for other people, and now here you are the one with a migraine."

"I don't get physically drained when I do a healing," she said. "I wear a mirror necklace." She points to her chest, revealing a gorgeous necklace with a mirrored circle in the center. "It's all about protection. I teach this to my students, too. You have to put up boundaries. I rarely do hands-on healings or readings anymore, either. I like to teach classes now and help others discover their gifts. The reason I stopped doing healings was because all the drama of all the people brought me down. People with cancer and tumors, and after years of doing about four healings a day, I said 'I can't do this anymore.' I was just fried. So now, you know what I do is, if I'm around somebody that is sick, and they haven't said anything to me, my hand just goes right to them. I'll put my hand on their shoulder or something and say, 'Oh, excuse me!' so I can give them some healing—maybe at the grocery store or something. I shoot the healing in and BOOM. So people get a healing without me having to get really involved in it."

"Tell me about your angel guides," I asked. "Do they change?"

"About every five years or so I get a different guide," Echo said. "Lilli came around about seven or eight years ago. She looks like Glinda the Good Witch in *The Wizard of Oz*. She's just a sweetheart. I don't rely on her for healing my headache or anything. She shows up when I work, and when I teach, she's usually off to the side. She's adorable and tells me what I forgot to tell the students. Then she disappears after class."

"I have a question about free will," I said. "If you see something coming in for someone that is a couple months out, like you mentioned my work projects and a possible love interest, can free will still derail that train?"

"Oh, yes, free will can mess it up, sure," she said.

Shit!

"I might see something and then somebody decides to make a sharp left turn, and the whole trajectory changes," she said. "Also, if someone says, 'He's the one' . . . I have an example I want to share. Someone came to me for a reading, and she met a guy and she said, 'I just know he's the one. Will you look and see?' So her guides were there in the room, and I looked at them and they said, with a very serious tone but with some hesitation, 'Yeah, tell her it's Mr. Right.' And I thought, 'There's a little trepidation here,' but I told her what they said I should tell her. Then she comes back about six months later and says, 'That was the worst relationship of my life! Why did my guides say that?' So the guides came back and said, 'She had some heavy karma with him, and if we would have told her, 'The next six months are going to be hell,' she would have bailed. They said, the good news is she finished the karma with that guy and she won't have to deal with him again. Now she is ready to meet 'Mr. Right.' So it's the guide's job to steer us down roads to complete certain relationships.

"Even I had something like this happen to me. When I was young, twenty-three, I went to a psychic named Carlos and said, 'When am I going to meet my future husband?' and he said 'I see you meeting him in March and you're marrying him in December. It's going to go very fast!' So the following January, I go on a diet because I'm getting ready for this guy to show up, and NOTHING. So I go back to Carlos and told him, and he said, 'I didn't say what year, did I? I still see March and December.' So every March for

I don't know how many years, I'd wait and nothing would happen. Thirteen years later, when I'm writing out my wedding invitations in November for my December wedding, I went, 'Oh, my God! Carlos! I DID meet Jim in March!' It had been off my radar, but it turned out to be correct. Timing is so hard to predict."

"How do you feel about psychic kids?" I asked. "Are you encountering a lot of psychic kids in your work?"

"Oh, yes, all the time," Echo said. "I have clients who have four-year-olds, five-year-olds, six-year-olds saying their kids are seeing spirit and predicting the future. They ask if they should try to squash it. And I tell everybody, 'No, just treat it as if it's normal and read some books and tell them that they have your permission to come and talk to you anytime they have an experience.' I'm really lucky because I had a mom who was psychic, my brother, my sister, our dad—he definitely had psychic abilities—and my other brother also has psychic abilities but he became a Fundamentalist and so he doesn't really have anything to do with us."

"What do you say to those people who say this is the devil's work? Especially with your own brother? That's got to be heartbreaking," I asked.

"I tell them that they should get out of the Old Testament and get into the New Testament because there's this guy named Jesus who came along and told us about the gift of prophecy and said in Corinthians that the gift of prophecy comes from the Holy Spirit," Echo said. "And a lot of times they end up shutting up because they realize I've read the Bible."

At that moment, our food arrived. We packed it up and took it next door.

✢ ✢ ✢

The center felt very cozy, filled with quirky lamps and framed spiritual quotes on the walls. One room was set up with chairs, obviously where the classes take place. The other room had merchandise—crystals, candles, books, mirrored necklaces, sage, and anything one would expect from a Spiritual Development Center.

Echo got out some plates, silverware, and bottles of water. We sat at the table to enjoy our food, which I do admit was totally delicious.

As we grazed and talked, a sign for recycling mysteriously fell off the wall.

"You have an environmentally friendly ghost," I said, going to pick up the "Please Recycle" sign.

"Do you have any ghosts here?" Marie asked.

"Well, we do have a ghost meter," Echo said in a matter-of-fact tone as if *everybody* had a ghost meter. "Let me turn it on."

Echo got up and turned a switch on a device on a nearby shelf.

"Now see, the light goes off if there's spirit energy that comes in here," she said.

Gotcha.

"Do you ghost bust anymore?" I asked. Echo and her brother Michael were known for making house calls to those places where things go bump in the night.

"Sometimes," she said. "There's a high school here in town, and a lot of people were seeing this teacher that had died. So I went over there, and there was one kid, he was a spirit, a ghost. And I asked him what his name is and he said 'Raymond.' And I asked, 'Are there a lot of you here?' and he said, 'Yes.' So I said, 'Can you go round everybody up and bring them in the auditorium and let's just talk?' And he did."

"They were all ghosts of kids that had died previously?" asked Marie.

"Yes," Echo said. "Teenaged ghosts are very interesting because they all say the same thing, 'Heaven is going to be boring. We're gonna get there, we're gonna get angel wings and what do we do, play a harp all day? I don't wanna go. I want to party and stay with my friends. I just want to be with people my age.' That's why the high school attracts so many teenaged spirits because they want to be around people their own age. After a while they just get restless. They want some action. They want people to know they're there, so that's why they start doing their little antics.

"So that night I asked Raymond, 'Could you be the ring leader here and I want everybody to hold hands and I want you all to go up [to the light] at the same time.' We did find the teacher, and we asked her to go up, too. And so what we saw was this whole group of kids holding hands and they all went up to the light together. It was really cool."

Not your typical day at the office.

"Why was the teacher hanging out at the school if she wasn't a teenager?" I asked.

"She passed from cancer and told me, 'This is my life. These kids are my kids. What am I gonna do in Heaven?' I said, 'You can be a teacher over there.' And she said, 'I can?' It never occurred to her. A lot of it is just educating these souls because they don't know what to think about death. That's our job to just let them know."

"Who do you go to for readings?" I asked.

"My brother Michael," she said. "He's so funny. He's nine years younger."

"Can I meet him someday?" I asked.

"Absolutely!" Echo said. "When you come back for a class, we will arrange it."

"Jen was telling me about the exit points or branch points that you write about in your book, and that we have a lot of times when we can choose to exit," Marie said.

In *What Happens When We Die*, Echo writes that each soul has certain "exit points" or moments in their life when they can either stay on earth or go back "home," depending on whether they've fulfilled their soul contracts. Some souls have several exit points and some only have one, meaning their death is literally "written in stone."

"So I'm curious about my son," Marie continued. "It seemed like it was possibly his time. . . . So when he was born, was this his predestined time?"

"How did he die?" Echo asked.

"A car accident," she said. "He was a passenger."

"Yeah, that would have been part of his life path, to live that little amount of time," Echo said. "Sometimes they'll say in their life path that they want their death to be a meaningful death for humanity. Like the people that died in the bombing in Brussels, their deaths will be part of history. Other people need to have a quiet death or sudden death. The timing of all of it, our birth and our death, is very important . . ."

"Is there ever a wrong place at the wrong time?" I asked.

"I've never seen one," Echo said.

"Even with my son, he had a premonition that he was not going to live to be twenty-five," Marie said. "He told several people. And I had a premonition that he was going to die."

"It had to be his time," Echo said. "I don't think I've ever seen someone die when it wasn't their time. But some of these ghosts are not accepting it. Most of the ghosts that I have met are really young souls. They aren't even aware that they have a life plan. The Elders make their life plan. So when they die, they don't say 'Oh, this was my life plan,' they're like, 'What do I do now?' So those are the guys who remain earthbound and become ghosts."

"So can I assume my son is with my parents even if he never met them?" Marie asked.

"Oh, yeah," Echo said. "We live with our families on the other side. . . . People always say, 'I'm sad my mom didn't get to meet her before she was born,' but it's like, 'Are you kidding? They hang out.' If they're a soul that's going to be born into that family, all the relatives on the other side go and hang out with that soul and tell the soul all about that family and their family history. And it's important to the soul, too. The soul does this little research on the family.

That's why you hear stories about little children who point to grandpa's picture and will say, 'Oh, that's grandpa. I met him in Heaven.' Little kids talk like it's so natural. There's no doubt in my mind your mom spent time with your son before he came in. It's really cool the way it all works."

"Do our loved ones send us signs?" Marie asked.

"They do," Echo said. "When I see a cardinal, I think of my mom. They usually will send something that makes us think of them right away when we see it. Is there anything that your son would send to you that you would know right away that it's him?"

Just then, the light on the ghost meter flashed.

"Maybe that means Joe is here?" I said, secretly hoping that Echo's "Spidey Senses" were back in action. "Are you feeling up to this?"

"I'm waiting for the door to open," Echo said, rubbing her head and closing her eyes.

After some small talk and clearing of dishes, Echo stood up.

"Okay, I'm going to walk in the back and get some coffee," she said. "I'll be back."

A few minutes later, Echo returned to the table.

Is this thing on?

She closed her eyes and began talking. Her pace was quick and determined, as if she was getting a download.

"Lilli said to tell you (Marie) that you've lived many lifetimes here on earth and you've also been male in a lot of your past lives. You have a very inventive kind of soul who likes to invent. Your soul has wanted to be here throughout history to create something new for humanity. You came into this lifetime as a female because you felt that women are now progressing more than men and you wanted to touch humanity in a different way in this lifetime. You didn't come in to be an inventor of things as much as you came in to be an inventor of ways to help humans advance. Hold on now."

Echo continued to close her eyes as Marie and I exchanged a look of excitement that the line to Lilli seemed to be open. While I certainly didn't know if Marie liked to invent things as Echo had mentioned, the male energy piece totally made sense. Not that Marie was masculine looking by any means, but her "get it done or else" kind of attitude with the reservations specialist at the Four Points Sheraton was very, well, masculine!

"She says that Ireland was one of your favorite past lives," Echo said. "You've had lifetimes in Ireland three different times, and she says your soul always likes to go back to Ireland. She says your soul was ambivalent about coming into this lifetime because it had been a while since you were a female and yet your soul was pretty excited about all of this—being a female, being a mother, being successful in business. And the key word for you is inventions: starting something new, creating something for mankind. Being a part of what makes the world tick. That is the most important role of your soul this lifetime."

At that moment, the ghost buster light went off again.

"She says your soul enjoys being female. But there's an image of your soul, there's a little frustration inside. Being female is a very different. . . . You know what people expect from men because of having a lot of incarnations as male, but you came in to experience the whole experience of being female, yet there is still a lot of masculine energy; like you're very much in your mind, your brain, your intellect, very practical, down-to-earth, I want to make a difference, I want to make a difference! This is how you are. . . . Some sort of bridging a gap. Making a difference. How am I going to make an impact like I have before? There's a down-to-earth, practical side to you that wants to shine and not in an egotistical way because you're way past that. You understand what that's about. . . . You know all about ego, and that's not where you're coming from in this life. You've just moved on from there."

Echo then went on to say that Marie would have two relationships. The first would be coming soon and last only seven months, and the second would be long lasting and would show up when she's fifty-two with someone who is disciplined, down-to-earth, grounded, supportive of her career, great in the kitchen, sweet, and wise with money.

Lucky!

"She says that your son has found himself a love on the other side," Echo said. "It's very sweet."

Both Marie and I sat up straight, excited that Joe had finally shown up.

"And she says it was definitely his time to go because his soul yearned for love and the one that he was going to fall in love with was already on the other side. He's very happy," Echo sat silently for a few moments. "I asked if he was able to come here, and she smiled and said, 'Oh, he's quite busy.'

He's got a very full life on the other side. He's doing very well. He has a lot of friends. I get an image of a young man, and he's walking down the street and he's smiling. There are a lot of people; his heart looks wide open. Because he is in love, his heart is very open and giving to people. He also works with welcoming young men, young people over, especially young guys his age who died quickly. He helps them when they come over because some of them were so absolutely unprepared, whereas he was prepared. And you're right, he really did know, he knew ever since he was little that he would not have a long life. He came, he got what he needed, and he was gone. And now he's on the other side, and she says he's a very busy young man. He goes and retrieves young souls who died in accidents like he did. He'll get an assignment—so and so is going to pass today in a car accident—and I see someone handing him the address of the accident, and he brings a lot of these souls over to the other side and then he talks to them. He explains to them what has happened. She said he's very good with them because some of them freak out, and he's just really calm about it. Takes them all over. Shows people all of the bene-fits of being home. Oh, that's cool. She said he actually had it written in his life plan that he wanted to go out like that because then his ultimate goal was to end up being a guide for people who pass that way. He's actually right where he wanted to be."

Once again, the ghost light started blinking.

"She said you'd be very, very proud of him for all the good that he's done since he's been there."

Marie silently wiped a tear.

Echo then switched to some career insights for Marie, and after a few moments, she asked, "She wants to know if you have any questions?"

Marie paused and thought for a moment.

"Are my mom or my dad available? I guess Joe's too busy with all of his friends and his girlfriend and his job," she said with a disappointed laugh.

Echo closed her eyes, and once again, the phone lines went dead.

"What's interesting is it went back to being blank like it was when we first tried to do this," she said. "I don't get this."

Damn you, crows!

"Well then, another question is I wonder why I keep coming back?" Marie asked.

"The reason that we even have reincarnation is because each lifetime is another attempt to reaching our highest potential. Your main life goal is *what and how much can I achieve as a female in this lifetime and then teach others how to do the same thing*," she said.

After the session, Echo opened her eyes.

"Did any of that resonate for you?" Echo asked.

Marie mentioned how she found it interesting that she had been a male many times, but that she didn't connect with the inventing piece. She admitted to loving Ireland and wanting to "make a difference" for people, and she wasn't surprised to hear that Joe is helping as many people on the other side as he helped in his short life. She was glad to hear he is happy, but sad that he was too busy to come and say hello.

"I think Joe always did want love that he never experienced on this earth, truly," she said, with a pensive look on her face. "He dated but not really. I guess I didn't realize you have romantic relationships in Heaven."

"Oh, yes, there are definitely love relationships on the other side," said Echo. "He looked really busy and really happy."

The next morning, we drove home and saw the aftermath of the storm that had hit the day before. Several semi trucks were still in ditches, and there were spinouts all over the road.

"We are so lucky we missed the worst of it," I said, clutching the wheel.

During our drive, Marie and I re-listened to her reading.

"I have to tell ya, I started to chuckle a little bit when she said you had had many lives as a male because when you were on the phone yesterday with all those hotels, all I could think was, 'Damn, that girl has balls!'" I said.

"Oh, that's too funny," she said.

"That's cool what she said about Ireland," I said.

"I look Irish," she said. "That could have been a guess."

To me, an Irish stereotype is someone with blonde or red hair and green eyes. Marie had dark hair and hazel eyes, but I would never describe her as someone who "looks Irish."

"How about her description of Joe?" I asked. "She talked about him the exact way you did to me on the car ride up."

"She could have said that to anyone about their son," she said shrugging it off.

I could sense Marie's skeptic taking center stage.

"My son has a couple of close friends and likes to go on walks in the woods and look for birds," I said. "She described someone who was the life of the party with hundreds of friends who is willing to take on big responsibilities. That's not everybody's son."

We drove in silence for a while—the bright sun causing a glare on the snow that even my sunglasses could not ease. The crows continued to show up in large amounts, both in trees and flying over the car. The sounds of Echo's voice came through the speakers, telling us that Marie may someday write a book and how she could get a bump up in her work situation in the fall. Then came the glowing description of the "evolved" man who will be showing up when Marie turns fifty-two.

"Well, at least I can look forward to a guy who gets me who can also cook," she said with a laugh.

"I wonder if he has a brother," I said.

3

The Other Bodines

WHEN WE RETURNED FROM MINNEAPOLIS, I listened to Echo's reading again and got this urge to learn more about her entire family. I looked up her brother Michael and ordered his book *Growing Up Psychic: From Skeptic to Believer*. I finished it in two days.

The tone of Michael's memoir was unlike any psychic book I'd ever read—rude, skeptical, and totally hilarious. From the age of seven, Michael's mother dragged him to every medium, psychic fair, and healing camp within a three hundred-mile radius. She opened her home to visiting mediums and psychics coming through the area, which allowed Michael and his siblings the opportunity to learn more about their own intuitive skills.

While Michael preferred to run away from the paranormal at lightning speed, his mother and sister Echo were totally onboard the "Woo-Woo Train to Psychic Town."

The Bodine family soon got the reputation for being "devil worshippers" and "psychic freaks," which made high school a bit challenging. Michael turned to partying to cope, which eventually landed him in rehab. What with his spirit guide Jerry trying to inhabit his body, the moaning Ouija board that moved stuffed animals, and enough drugs and alcohol for all of Minnesota, Michael experienced more before his sixteenth birthday than most people do their entire lives.

I got his contact info from Echo and called him up to see if he'd be willing to read me and an anonymous friend.

"Shit yes, let's do this," he said.

I love this guy!

The friend I chose to bring with me was Lisa Dietlin—one of my "Remarkable Woman" subjects from my days as a columnist at the *Chicago Tribune*. As a philanthropy expert and author of several books, Lisa works hard, plays hard, and then works harder. Her book *I Got Hit By a Taxi, But You Look Run Over* tells the story of the epiphany she had after a cab going thirty-five miles per hour hit her in the Chicago Loop. She was knocked clear out of her shoes but survived the incident without a scratch. When she was in the hospital waiting for her test results, she heard an inner voice say clearly in her ear, "It's all bullshit except happiness and joy." Since that moment, she's been slowly but surely doing her best to incorporate happiness and joy into her everyday life.

We drove to Minneapolis on a Friday morning in April. Lisa was going to pick me up at 5:30 a.m. so we could make it in time for one of Echo's classes at 12:30.

She pulled up at 5:31.

"Sorry I'm one minute late," she said, putting my overnight bag in her back of her jeep.

Lisa really likes to be on time.

Another reason I thought she would be the perfect person to take on my latest paranormal adventure is that Lisa lost her father Robert when she was just thirteen years old. He was canoeing with a friend and Lisa's younger brother Jeff in Montana when the boat tipped over and hit a whirlpool. Robert saved her brother and went back in to save the friend. Both Robert and his friend drowned. While it had happened thirty-nine years ago, the pain of losing her father so young still feels like yesterday for Lisa.

We were on the schedule to see Michael the afternoon we arrived and would visit his other sister Nikki the following morning.

"Echo said that Nikki does medium stuff but no psychic stuff," I said while getting our GPS all ready for the long drive. "Michael is a future guy but doesn't like to talk to dead people unless he's doing a ghost-busting job."

I sounded like a producer of some crazy show on TLC.

"I think I've got it straight," Lisa said.

As the sun started to rise, I saw several dozen red-winged blackbirds in trees along the highway. There were so many that it made me take notice.

"Are you seeing all those red-winged blackbirds?" I asked.

"Birds are your thing, not mine," she joked since all of my friends know I see cardinals when I'm thinking about my deceased father. "I like words. License plates, signs, etc."

Just then, a car with the license plate ENUFFF got in front of us.

"See?" she said, pointing to the car.

I picked up my phone and decided to ask Siri about the birds.

"Siri, show me the spiritual meaning of the red-winged blackbird," I said.

"Let me take a look," Siri said.

"You made Siri an Australian guy?" Lisa asked with a laugh.

"A New Zealand guy!" I said. "Okay, here we go. The red-winged blackbird is letting you know that the forces of nature are at work and that big changes are coming into your life right now. These changes have been slowly manifesting all around you and are now ready to burst forth and become reality."

"Hell yes!" Lisa said.

Both she and I had gone through significant work changes over the past few months with many projects in the hopper. The idea that some of them would "burst forth" sounded very appealing.

Several more license plates made their presence known over the next couple of hours. "2 FUN" and "FUNHOG" made us giggle. And then we were back to the birds.

"Holy shit!" I said, pointing to a field of at least seventy-five geese.

"I don't think I've ever seen so many geese in one spot," Lisa said.

Back to Siri.

"The goose carries the magical totem powers of synchronicity," I said, reading from my phone.

At that moment we saw about three dozen geese flying over the highway.

"The goose leads you to your heart's desire or your treasure. If the goose shows up, it means you are finding or nearing your purpose in life, that which gives you bliss. The more geese in the flock, the nearer to your treasure and heart's desire you become."

After seeing thirteen red-tailed hawks ("intuition, wisdom, and spiritual awareness") and a bald eagle that swooped over our sunroof ("rising above the material to see the spiritual"), we were officially birded out.

And then, it was time for our exit into Minneapolis.

"Robert Street!" Lisa yelled, pointing to the name of our exit.

Sure enough, we had to exit on Robert Street to get to our destination.

"Good one, Dad," she said.

That's weird!

We rolled into town just in time to grab a quick bite at Huey's next door to the center, where I'm happy to report the fried rice was still great and the food was still made fresh to order. After lunch, it was time to head to Echo's Intuition Support Group.

Every Friday, she gathers people to discuss their highs and lows of trying to incorporate intuition into their daily lives. Lisa and I sat in the seats and did our best to fit in to the group of about twenty loyal class regulars made up of nineteen women and one man. On this spring day, it was a balmy seventy-seven degrees, so there was no worry of bad weather shutting the doors.

Echo stood in front of the class and smiled as she opened her arms to the room.

"This is an intuition support group where we talk about listening to our intuition, how it turned out, and if we didn't listen to our intuition and how *that* turned out," Echo said. "Then at the end we have a meditation. Would anyone like to start?"

A woman raised her hand.

"My dad had some tests done, and we went to the doctor and he got a stress test done. And the doctor said, 'The reports look okay, so come back in six months.' But my intuition said, 'No, something is not okay!' And it said that again and again. So I insisted that we take him to the cardiologist next door, and the cardiologist said, 'He already had a heart attack!' And they did more tests and found he had five blockages in his heart. They had to do a bypass."

Several people in the room gasped.

"Good job!" Echo said, starting to clap, which led into a full round of applause from the class.

The woman beamed as if she'd just announced several years of sobriety to an AA meeting.

"A lot of people in my family were upset with me because they thought I was making it up and being too sensitive," she added. "I just kept saying, 'I know he's not well.'"

"Did we get to the 'Rocking the Boat' chapter?" Echo asked.

I noticed several people in the group holding Echo's book on intuition entitled *A Still Small Voice.*

"That was last week's chapter," someone said, flipping through the pages.

"When you just know that something isn't right but everything around us says, 'Are you making this up? Why are you trying to be dramatic?' it can be really tough to stand up for your intuition, so you have to be strong and hold your ground. Your intuition is *always* right," Echo said.

On our way to Michael's house, Lisa and I both felt a nervous anticipation.

"I am dying to meet this guy," I said.

No pun intended.

We parked in front of a modest-sized house in Edina, Minnesota, and made our way down the long sidewalk to the front door. I looked around the lawn and noticed several stone statues of fairies placed around the yard. I also saw a pile of Halloween decorations stacked near some bushes.

Maybe they celebrate Halloween all year long?

Just then, a very tall, blond man with light eyes approached us from around the side of the house. He had energy coming out of his fingertips.

"Great to see you," said Michael, hugging me.

I felt like I'd known him my entire life.

Michael is in his mid to late fifties but looks to be about forty-five, with the essence of a thirty-year-old after two pots of coffee. He wore jeans, black cowboy boots, and a black long-sleeved shirt. As he talked, he kept pushing his long hair back, which frequently fell in front of his eyes.

"Let's go in," he said, opening the front door.

His blond hair and distinguished face reminded me of Rod Stewart from his married to Rachel Hunter era.

Once inside, we were greeted by a small dog.

"He's blind and deaf, so he won't hurt you," Michael said as the dog barked at the opposite wall.

There were purple and white Christmas lights draped throughout the entryway and living room and fairy statues on every table. The walls were covered with beautifully framed photos of his kids, Blake and Bianca.

"Your children are gorgeous," I said.

"I fucking LOVE my kids!" he said, widening his eyes. "Seriously, there is nothing I love more than my kids."

I'd been in his presence for a mere thirty seconds, and he'd already dropped the f-bomb.

I'm with my people!

We made our way into the kitchen, which I could tell was used by someone who loves to cook. And then there were the dozens of cans of different kinds of tomato sauce stacked on the counter. I stopped counting at fifty.

"Umm . . . is someone making some sauce?" I asked.

"Oh, yeah," he said. "I went to culinary school for two years, so I love to cook and bake."

Next to the kitchen was the family room, which had an antique wooden bar against the wall complete with bottles of liquor that likely hadn't been touched since Ronald Reagan was in office. Near the unused booze were stacks of old VHS tapes. On the walls, more pictures of the kids from all ages.

"Do your children have the gift, too?" I asked. Michael wrote in his book about his son having a psychic sensitivity from a very young age.

"Blake comes with me on the ghost busting," he said, pushing his hair out of his eyes. "My mom would teach him stuff when I would drop him off to have her babysit. Bianca is learning to read peoples' minds now, but I'm hoping she's just going to be normal. This is such a dumb job. But Blake is really good at doing readings."

I looked down and saw a black cat.

Of course.

"Who is this?" I said, reaching down to give it a scratch on the head.

"Oh, that's Bagheera," he said. "Named after the panther in *The Jungle Book*."

As I got closer, I noticed he only had three legs.

You can't make this shit up!

"He doesn't really like to be touched, so be careful," he said as the cat gave me a not-so-nice look.

I slowly backed away without making any sudden moves.

Don't mess with me, Bagh-whatever-your-name-is.

Lisa decided to go first for her reading. Michael knew nothing about her, except her first name.

"Have fun, kids," I said as they shut the door to Michael's office.

I grabbed my copy of Echo's intuition book and sat in a lounge chair by the front window to enjoy the fresh air. Within seconds, the blind, deaf dog jumped up on the chair with me.

I heard cardinals singing as I dug into Echo's book. The house soon became soothing to me as the unseasonably warm breeze hit my face. The only interruption to this blissful state was the occasional sound of Lisa's laughter, which is so vibrant I often describe it as "the laugh that could stop traffic."

Suddenly, I heard a sound I couldn't quite recognize.

"Bang, bang, BOOM. Bang, bang, BOOM."

I looked around to see if perhaps one of Michael's kids had come in the back door, but nobody was there. Out of the corner of my eye, I saw a figure dragging itself on the floor in my direction. As my heart rate increased, I put on my glasses to take a closer look.

Is this house haunted?

It was that damned three-legged cat slowly making his way to my chair. Before I could get my bearings to stand up, he leapt onto my lap and landed with an awkward thud. He rotated around several times to get comfortable, found the perfect spot to perch, and plopped down. Within minutes he started purring.

I surrender.

Apparently, I'm a three-legged-cat whisperer.

An hour and change later, Lisa and Michael made their way out of the office.

"Now remember, tell everyone that I suck, okay?" Michael joked.

Lisa smiled at me, grabbed her purse and her phone, and went to the front room as I entered Michael's office.

"Come on in!" he said, popping a piece of chocolate candy in his mouth.

The room where Michael did his work looked like something out of the Ripley's Believe It Or Not! Museum; everything was black and purple, with skulls, fairies, crystals, more fairies, and more skulls.

I sat on the couch and Michael sat next to me, which sort of surprised me.

"Hi, honey!" he said, like we were old buddies.

"Hi!" I said, getting comfortable.

"So I'm a basic psychic kind of guy—a future guy. I don't spin or levitate or anything like that," he said, grabbing his notebook and a pen. "All I need from you is what you want to know about—what areas. Once we start, I can't ask you any questions. You can ask me whatever you want, but I can't ask you stuff."

I didn't tell Michael anything about me, and he claimed he didn't do any research, which of course I had no way of confirming.

"Well, one thing I'd like to know about is my love life," I said.

"Is there anyone in your life right now?" he asked getting his pen ready.

"Nope."

Michael stopped writing and looked me square in the eyes. After a few beats, he broke the stare and went back to his notebook.

"Interesting," he said, not looking up from his paper as he scribbled.

I wondered what thoughts were popping into his mind.

"They did you a favor on that deal," he said, still writing. "Ending that last relationship. They had to clear the decks. But okay, what else?"

Clear the decks?

"Work stuff would be good, too," I said.

Michael continued to write and look off to the side as if someone was talking to him.

"Oh, honey, yeah," he said. "Yeah. Uh huh. Yeah, of course. Yeah."

"Are you hearing things or seeing things?" I asked.

"I'm talking to your guides and they show me pictures—it's like they open up a movie," he said. "It's like going through a bunch of files and they're showing me all this stuff about you, and I know that you talk to other psychics, so I don't want to bore you, but honey, you have a sweetheart coming."

Hot diggity!

"You must get sick of psychics," he said with a laugh, putting down his notebook. "And I'm sure people have told you about the tsunami that's coming into your life— the complete change. Stevie Wonder can see it, it's not like you have to dig that deep! Things are about to blow up for you. Your writing is great, and there's a whole bunch of stuff coming up for you in different ways. New things. Things that have to do with entertainment and a TV show."

Unbeknownst to Michael I had a movie script, TV show pitch, and documentary project all floating in the ethers.

He looked off to the side and started to talk but stopped himself. Then he laughed, smiled, and laughed again.

"Yeah, shut up!" he said, talking to the wall.

As I was watching him mouth off at my spirit guides, I got the most intense feeling of déjà vu.

"Are you filtering yourself?" I asked.

"It's weird with you because I *know* you. We've talked before. I know you. It's kind of like talking to my sister or a girlfriend. Somebody I've known for a long time. You're extremely familiar to me."

I knew it!

"Okay, so back to your work," he said, trying to shake off whatever movie they showed him that revealed we were once related. "Honey, you have a job here to do and with the success that's coming to you . . . the test now is how you are going to handle all the stuff that is about to hit for you. Are you going to stay true to yourself? I don't know. Being alone has been hard on you. I think everything has been taken out of your way so there is no resistance because you're ready and they need you to be ready for what's coming without anything or anyone weighing you down."

I remembered Echo using the analogy of the "weights around my neck" had I stayed in my previous relationship.

He looked off to the side and then pushed his hair out of his eyes.

"What the fuck were you thinking with your last boy-friend?" he asked. "You must have been bored. I mean you can't do boring, honey. This guy was like Mr. Rogers."

OMG!

"You're going to like what's coming in for you, though," he continued. "They said this person who is coming is equal to you. They *love* your work. They want to do a lot of cool things. There's a lot of passion, but you're teaming up on a mental level, too. You need that. But the love interest isn't going to come right away. Your dead guys have you in posi-tion now to do some pretty cool stuff, and you can't be dis-tracted with a passionate love right now. You're their bitch, and they have plans for you."

And there's the title for my next book.

"They've had to suppress you. They are pulling back this rubber band and they're going to let it go, and it all happens really fast—relationships, book deals, you'll be doing stuff in Los Angeles. Everything is going to change with you, your hairstyle, your makeup, your clothes. Everything."

Does that mean I get to go shopping?

"But, honey, you just suck at relationships," he said.

"The people I *choose* suck," I said, feeling defensive. "I love hard, and I don't get it back sometimes."

"Sometimes?! Shit! *Most* times. You're intense and pas-sionate. You love hard, and you go for a person's potential. Even that narcissist you had before Mr. Rogers had poten-tial. You need someone who at least has spark, and he had a spark, that's for sure."

How did he know the guy I dated before Jason had a spark? Oh, yeah, he's psychic.

"It was supposed to work out with Jason," he said, looking up at the sky. "I know, shut up! Yeah, I got it. His feelings for you were absolutely true. You were it. But he wasn't ready to move forward."

Story of my life.

"You are the one that got away," he said. "You will hear from him again. But don't go back with him. Your guides are begging you. Because you are so depleted right now, you might be tempted. You need to get your body out of the red zone."

Michael put his hands together like he was clapping and then held them out in my direction.

"Oh, for the love of God, turn around, I have to put this heat on you," he said.

The next thing I knew, Michael spun me around and put his hands on my shoulder blades. They were so hot, it felt like two irons were being placed on my back. I closed my eyes and started seeing blue and green flashes of light. The energy coming from his hands almost knocked me over.

"How old were you when you knew you could heal with your hands?" I asked, trying not to melt into the couch.

"When I was about eight," he said. "Both Echo and Nikki do healing work, but I usually don't because I can't stand touching people. But my hands got hot as soon as you sat down, and they said you really need this."

Yes . . . I . . . do.

"Your son, by the way, he's very tuned in. And he's very protected," he said, still sending heat into my back. "He's going to visit Normandy, which will be very healing for him."

I couldn't believe he mentioned Normandy. My son Britt is obsessed with World War II. I'm convinced he had a past life fighting the Germans. He always talks about wanting to go to the "beaches of Normandy."

Can't Google that!

"He doesn't care much for the lack of manners in this century," he said. "His soul struggles with this time."

My child is ten going on 150.

"He's going to be very tall, too," he added. "And have a deep voice."

Michael took his hands off my back and turned me around.

"Your body is kind of screwed up, and you need a good massage," he said.

I concur!

"It's gone without for too long. It needs attention. Not just alignment but loving touch. Do this every week. Not just once a month. They can talk to you then, too, when you're on the massage table. They need you glowing like ET, and they need you in shape and ready to go. And that's their plan for the summer. That's when the big relationship comes, too. If you got excited about fish-and-chips, honey, just you wait! You're going to really like what's coming. I mean *'Hello!'* It elevates everything."

I hope he's right!

"So tell me about the ghost busting stuff you do?" I asked, remembering I had a job to do to learn as much about Michael as possible. "Don't you think that exposes you to a lot of dark energies?"

"Oh, no, they don't scare me," he said. "We have an agreement—I don't screw with their stuff, they don't screw with me. In some cases, they're overstepping their bounds, and you just have to negotiate with them. I think people who are afraid of that stuff bring in more activity. The ghosts feed on the fear. When I teach a ghost busting class, the whole point is to talk about the fears of the people who own the house. I want people to be able to go in there under any circumstances and not be afraid, so if the walls are bleeding or the cats are flying around—which happens, not that often but it does happen—I want to show people how to stay through their fears. The dead people I have a problem with are suicides or drug overdoses. They're afraid to go to the other side because they're afraid they'll be judged or punished. Some of them don't even know they're dead."

"So your mom and Echo were embracing all this stuff when you were growing up, but how did your dad take it?" I asked.

"My dad was in denial about it," he said. "My mother kept it alive. She dove into it. Her family was full of gypsies on her side. And shit was always happening to the house with the ghosts. Nikki didn't get into it until later. And my older brother is a Fundamentalist and doesn't want anything to do with us because he thinks we're all the Devil."

As Michael was talking, I noticed a large gold cross around his neck.

"You were raised Baptist, so do you go to church now?" I asked.

"I'm not a fan of many people who go to church, but I love God," he said. "There is a light and a dark, and I just believe in the light. If you've ever seen the movie *Constantine* with Keanu Reeves, a lot of that movie was actually true. When a person is possessed, you put a mirror in front of them and you use different religious things for different cases. I mean if you walk into a haunted house and wield the cross and the spirit is Jewish, they'll be like, 'Yeah, whatever!' That cross won't have any impact. You have to know what you're doing."

"You wrote that you lost your gift for a stretch," I said. "What happened?"

Michael took a deep breath and pushed his hair out of his eyes.

"Yeah. Back in the eighties I was this cocky psychic. I was so accurate, and I didn't even care. I wasn't taking care of the gifts or honoring them. I was reading celebrities and featured in all these magazines, and I started thinking, 'Wow, I'm a pretty amazing guy.' And one day I was doing this local radio show on WCCO and I was doing a reading for the DJ and all this stuff is coming through—this is live on the radio—and I'm saying to him, 'People don't like you these days at work,' and 'Your son is struggling,' and it was coming through clear as a bell and he was like, 'I don't have sons, I have daughters, and things couldn't be better at work.' Everything I told him was wrong. Everything. He was looking at me like, 'Dude, come up with *something*.' And the voice that was giving me all the information was the same voice that had given me the right stuff before, so it was very confusing for me. Then at the end he looks at me and hands me a twenty-dollar bill and says, 'Here, I think you're going to need this!'"

"That's horrible," I said.

"And my teacher—her name was Birdie—she came down to the station and was standing there when I walked out, and she said, 'You have to come down a few pegs.' And I lost the gift for about a year. Everything I said for a year was wrong. So yeah, that was a wake-up call for me. I don't like the psychic stuff very much, but I really don't want to lose it again."

"Can you still astral travel?" I asked.

One of my favorite moments in Michael's book explains how his soul took a field trip to his seventh-grade crush's bedroom one night while he was sleeping. A very excited Michael told her the next day at school, complete with a description of her "night gear" retainer and what she wore to bed. Needless to say, it didn't go over too well.

"I'll astral travel, but only when necessary," he said with a smile.

"You also think that Ouija boards are bad news," I said, recalling another story from his book.

"Say you're dead and you're not in the light and you're bored, so you want to scare people," he said. "All of the sudden you see this little light, and there are these people around it asking questions like 'Does Billy like me?' So the dead people think, 'Hey, I think I'll fuck with these people! Why not?!' And these low spirits go in and it gets darker and darker."

"But you were using it a lot in your house growing up, right?" I asked.

"You bet," he said. "We were using it to go to the grocery store! But we didn't know any better. We thought it was just another way to talk to the dead. Echo was playing with the board one night when she had a sleepover, and they were asking normal questions and then the vibe got really weird in the room. At around 3 a.m. all the lights started going on and off, and then the lights stay on and my sister's stuffed snake that was draped over her bed starts going back and forth and it got so much momentum it flew off the bed. She was so freaked out! The parents came and got the kids. That's when people started calling us the 'Satan Family,' saying we lived in a haunted house. So my mom decided we had to get rid of the Ouija board.

"The next day I came home from school, and I wanted to take out the thing to do it with Mary Joe Robinson because I wanted to get her to make out with me. So I'm looking all over for it, and I asked my mom where it was and she said 'It's gone. We can't even talk about it anymore.' After a while she told me what happened. My mom put it in the garbage outside, and when she came back into the house, the thing was on the table. She was totally freaked out. So then my mom decides she's going to burn it, and she tries and it doesn't burn! She finally had to pour accelerant on it to get it to burn. And when it was burning, it was moaning and crying, and it took forever. So, since then, our teachers have all said, stay away from them. Pendulums can do the same thing. It's giving them too much power. It's when you're not clear on what you want and you're just looking for any kind of sign, the chances of you getting what you want are pretty slim."

As Michael was talking, I heard a cardinal chirping outside.

"Driving up here today, I saw so many different birds," I said. "I see birds a lot, but this was more than usual."

"What do you think the messages were?" Michael asked.

You're the psychic, you tell me!

"Well, all the definitions we found of what the birds represented were pretty accurate to what I'm up to right now, I have to admit," I said.

"And what do you think it means in the big picture? Usually there is a big picture in all this," he said, looking at me with intensity.

I thought about Dr. Mary Neal.

"That signs are all around us that we're never alone and that source is always in communication with us," I said, hoping to pass the test.

"It's time to take that message and bring it to other people," he said. "See, that's the frustration our guides have with dealing with humans—they will see the signs and say, 'What?! That's just a coincidence.' The first few times it might be coincidence, but after so many in a row you have to know it's bigger than that. You have to widen your perspective and really take this to the next level."

Lisa and I compared notes in the car on our way back to the hotel and found it interesting that we had quite a few similarities with our readings. Michael got that she was an author and that she was a "powerful force" in business. He also said that like me, she, too, was going to be "blowing up." She would be speaking in front of large crowds and writing more books. He said that she and I are both on a very specific mission and we belonged to the world. While my guides (I had four) didn't care for Jason, hers (she had five) thought her boyfriend Chris, who happened to be a firefighter, was "just fine." In fact, when he talked about Chris, a very loud fire truck can be heard on the audio recording in the background driving down the street.

But since Michael didn't like to talk to dead people, we were hoping our final Bodine encounter might produce a message from Robert.

The next morning, we grabbed bagels and coffee and headed to Nikki's house.

"GPS says it's four minutes away," I said as I plugged the address into the phone.

Nikki had only been given Lisa's first name and nothing else.

"I'm so excited!" she said as we started to drive.

We arrived in front of a beautiful white farmhouse. No stone fairies. No Halloween decorations. Just a pristine lawn in front of a cozy home.

Nikki greeted us at the door, and her bright eyes took my breath away.

"Look at those green eyes!" I said, giving her a hug.

"Aren't these contacts fun?" she said, blinking her eyelashes over her stunning green eyeballs.

Nikki had a petite frame and brown hair with blonde bangs in the front. While I knew her age to be about sixty, she also seemed much younger than her years. Her demeanor was sweet, and her voice was soft and soothing.

She led us upstairs to the room where she does her work. Walking up the stairwell, I noticed pictures of angels, Jesus, and hearts. The prominent colors of her decorating were white, pink, and lavender.

She was the exact opposite of Michael.

We entered the room where we were going to have our reading, and she had us sit on a pink couch, complete with heart-shaped pillows. Nikki sat on a chair just across from us next to what looked to be a massage table that she likely used for her healing work.

"*Soooo* who are we contacting today?" she asked. While Michael and Echo didn't have much of a Minnesota accent, it seemed to leak out a bit when Nikki used the letter *o*. "I like to call on someone; I don't just sit here and see who comes."

I'd gotten so used to Thomas John's style of coming up with names without any prompting, I briefly forgot that not all mediums have the same ability.

"I'd like to call on my dad, Robert," Lisa said.

"That's all I need," she said. "And how long has he been gone?"

"It's been thirty-nine years in March," Lisa said.

"Oh, dear!" Nikki said. "The longer they're gone, the less they say sometimes. So we'll see."

Lisa and I exchanged a glance of "I hope this isn't a problem!" and settled into the pink cushions.

"You guys ready?" Nikki asked.

"Indeed!" Lisa said.

Nikki closed her eyes and took a few deep breaths.

"Sometimes it starts off slow," she said, immediately discounting her gifts. "All right. What I sense right away—and I will ask if this stuff resonates—but what I sense is a man, very strong. I sense a boat or a captain. I don't know if he liked boating or what this is, or if he liked the water or the sea? He feels like a captain. Does that make sense?"

Lisa and I exchanged a surprised look.

"He was an avid fisherman," Lisa said softly.

"Oh, well there you go—perfect. Thank you," Nikki said. "Definitely loved the water. There's something that he stands very proud. I see a hat on him. He's proud and standing tall. Was he gone a lot?"

"Yes, he worked a lot," Lisa said. "Double shifts."

"The kids—say 'hi' to the kids. And the grandkids. It feels like he has seen the grandkids and is watching them grow up," Nikki continued with her eyes closed. "He's here but I still sense him far away. He feels like a man who was loving, yet he didn't show a lot of his feelings. He was very matter-of-fact. He got the job done. He took care of you kids very well."

"Yes," Lisa said.

"Your mother. He's talking about your mother. He misses her," Nikki said. "I hear a word *T*—starts with a *T*. Two? I don't know what this is. Two? Someone have a name that starts with a *T*? If not, it's fine. Two. Something about that. I'm still practicing with names."

I looked at Lisa and she shrugged an "I don't know" as Nikki continued.

"I know everybody smoked back then, but I see something here in his lungs that affected his death. Is that true?" Nikki asked.

"He drowned," Lisa said.

"Okay—that makes sense," Nikki said. "I feel a heaviness in his lungs. I could tell his death was right here." She put her hand on her chest. "He's sorry about something. He's sorry he left you and left so early. He's sorry, but he didn't know any better at the time; he just worked like everybody works back then. He loved you dearly. And he misses you . . . He's proud of you and your success. You've come a long way and taken the right path and done what you needed to do to be able to heal in this life."

Lisa slowly wiped away a tear.

"Do you have a question for him?"

"Why did he go back in the water?" Lisa asked.

Nikki sat for a minute, tuning in.

"I hear the word 'save,'" she said. "Don't know what that means yet. That's a tough one. Save. I hear the word 'save.'"

"You nailed it because he went back in the water to save someone," Lisa said. "Is his brother Don with him?"

"Yeah, it feels like it," Nikki said. "Don—I'm laughing because his energy is totally different. He feels like a funny guy or laid-back, relaxed, kind of a silly guy. Those two get along and have fun together. When they were alive, it feels like they had a lot of differences, but now they're fine. Does that make sense?"

"That's completely true," Lisa said.

"They didn't see eye to eye, and your dad thought Don was kind of a doofus. Does that make sense? But now they're like this [fingers crossed]. Family was a lot to your dad. Love is the key. That's what he says. His brother says 'hi,'" Nikki said.

"Don was a big drinker and would get into fights at the bar, and my dad would have to go and get him out of these scrapes."

Suddenly, Lisa sat up as if she'd just remembered something important.

"I figured out what the *T* word is," Lisa said. "They both always called my mom 'Toots.'"

"You know, that sounds right!!" Nikki said, bouncing in her chair with excitement. "I kept hearing the *t* sound. Or 'two.' That's perfect, thank you for remembering that."

"Are they happy?" Lisa asked.

"Oh, yeah, they're very happy," Nikki said. "Dad is doing what he loves and watching the grandkids. He must be out there on the water still because that's where he feels happiest. They send their love."

Nikki then went on with a few more messages from Don about Lisa's mother's health and how Bob is hanging out with his ancestors. Eventually Nikki opened her eyes as if to signal that the coast was clear and exhaled.

"I hope that was okay," she said, folding her hands in her lap.

"Yes, thank you," Lisa said with relief.

"Oh, you're welcome!" Nikki said with a big smile.

"How long have you had this gift?" I asked.

"I didn't get this until I was forty," Nikki said. "I used to think Echo was crazy. I mean I saw ghosts when we were growing up in that house, but then when I moved out, I detached from them. Echo would tell me stuff and I'd be like, 'Yeah whatever!' I mean, especially if you read her books, it's like, 'Really, sis?' But now I believe in all of it."

"How did it start for you?" I asked.

"When I was forty, I was at a funeral of a friend of mine, and he came into the funeral home and said, 'Hi, Nikki, so nice to see you.' I was like, 'Huh????' That was the very first time I heard the deceased. I heard his voice. He was standing right next to me."

"So is it only audio or do you get visual, too?" I asked.

"It's both. I hear and see."

"Married? Kids?" I asked.

"Neither. I have a honey, but he's a traditional Catholic boy that doesn't really believe in this," Nikki said.

"I asked Echo if anyone's time is really the wrong time, and she said she hasn't really experienced that because she says you have these exit points of when you can go, even with suicide," I said. "What do you think? Is there a wrong place at a wrong time?"

"I don't know because in this work, they all seem okay on the other side," Nikki said. "Except the suicides in the beginning, they're really upset. That is where I could say it might not be the right time, but even when there is a freak accident, I've got to believe it's their time. Even the suicide victims are happy and healed a year later. But that might be a question we will never know."

After we left Nikki's, we headed over to Echo's "Aurapalooza" at the center. This is a monthly event with several vendors who do everything: numerology, acupuncture, psychic readings, and massage.

"It's like Christmas for the woo-woo crowd," I said.

We pulled out of Minneapolis shortly after getting our aura pictures taken, because, well . . . why the hell not.

"I'm so sad to leave," I said, looking at the gorgeous multicolored sunset in the rearview mirror.

While the mood during our drive up on Friday had been all laughs and joy, things were much more pensive on the commute home. Lisa was happy with the information Nikki had brought through, but there was a heaviness in the air.

"I keep my dad's hat in the back," Lisa said, with a serious look on her face. "The one he was wearing when he drowned."

"Wow," I said, surprised she'd never shared that with me before.

"It's my way of keeping him close," she said, looking straight ahead.

A few hours later we were making great time, and I noticed Lisa looking in the backseat like she saw something out of the corner of her eye.

"What is it?" I asked.

"Must be headlight reflections from the trucks," she said.

She looked into the rearview mirror and then in the backseat again. I was checking my phone for emails as she slowly leaned into the middle console like she had to tell me a secret.

"There's someone behind us," she said in a stage whisper, her eyes as wide as saucers.

I looked behind our car to see who might be tailing us.

"You mean on the highway?" I asked seeing no car in sight.

"No, I mean in the backseat," she said, still whispering.

Oh, shit!

Lisa is a practical businesswoman, not a medium. Hearing her say she suspected the backseat of her Jeep Cherokee was inhabited by a ghost was definitely unexpected.

I leaned in to her eye level.

"I'm guessing if there's a ghost back there, it can already hear us, so why are you whispering?" I asked.

Lisa let out a good laugh, and then, "I swear I saw something back there," she said now using her normal tone. "When I looked into the rearview mirror, I saw a smiling face. Get your camera phone and take some pictures of the backseat and see if you get any images."

Echo said digital cameras are great for picking up images of energy or even ghosts. I grabbed my phone and started clicking away but nothing showed up in the images. As I leaned back in my chair, I felt a squeeze on my right shoulder.

"Ahhhh!" I said, squirming as if a spider had bitten me.

"What is it?" Lisa asked.

"I just felt something squeeze my shoulder," I said, hoping it was all in my imagination.

Lisa suddenly jumped in her seat.

"OH, GOD!" She screamed. "I just felt something grab my left arm."

What the hell is going on here?!

I tried to center my breathing, remembering what Michael said about how ghosts get stronger the more afraid you become of them. Then it hit me.

Michael!

I picked up my phone and texted my new psychic friend.

"Where are you right now?" I wrote.

He responded immediately with "In your backseat."

Cue creepy music!

"I guess I need to be more discreet in my astral travel," he continued.

"It's Michael!" I yelled. "He traveled into the car!"

"What?!" Not having read Michael's book, Lisa was really confused.

"He can astral travel," I said as if this were a perfectly normal statement.

"Well tell him to cut it out," she said. "I'm trying to drive here!"

Michael then went on to text the he wanted to warn us that he saw some bad drivers up ahead and to be extra cautious.

Minutes later, there was a red car in front of us weaving all over the road, actually hitting the cement wall repeatedly. Lisa got as far away from that driver as possible.

"I guess it's nice to have psychic friends sometimes," I said.

"No kidding," she said.

"I swear the Bodines need their own TV show," I said.

"Or at least we should get a screenplay out of the last thirty-six hours!" Lisa said.

We decided that Annette Bening should play Echo, Meryl Streep would be a good Nikki, and either Brad Pitt or Leonardo DiCaprio would be perfect for Michael.

Lisa turned on the satellite radio and chose "Sounds of the '70s" for the home stretch as we tapped our toes to most of the *Saturday Night Fever* soundtrack.

The sky was quiet, and our minds were racing with all that we had seen and experienced in the last day and a half.

"I guess no matter how many mediums I meet who claim they're talking to dead people, it still doesn't bring them back, does it?" I said, looking at the stars.

"No, it sure doesn't," Lisa said.

On Monday, Lisa left me a voice mail.

"Hey there, I just wanted you to know, my mom called me this morning to tell me that my dad came to her and sat on the foot of her bed on Saturday night. He's never done that before. I hadn't told her about our trip, so I shared with her all that Nikki said about Dad on Saturday, too. She was pretty amazed. Isn't that wild? Okay, call me later, gator. Hugs!"

That's weird!

4

Rebecca Rosen

WHEN REBECCA ROSEN WAS A TWENTY-YEAR-OLD college student at the University of Florida, her life turned upside down one day when she started hearing her dead grandmother's voice. Rebecca was battling depression and writing in her journal when the energy took over her hand, and she couldn't write fast enough. The messages, she was told, were from her father's mother, who'd committed suicide when Rebecca was just ten years old.

Having never dipped her toe in the paranormal pond, she was extremely skeptical of the voice that was coming through. So Rebecca's dead grandmother told her to call her father and ask him three very specific questions that only he would know. One of those questions was about the way her dad found his mother after she had taken her life, which he'd kept to himself. She called her dad and gave him the messages, and he started to cry. He then told her that whatever was going on, she should just keep doing it.

Now in her late thirties and living in the Denver area, Rebecca is a full-time medium and author with two best sellers: *Spirited: Unlock Your Psychic Self and Change Your Life* and *Awaken the Spirit Within: 10 Steps to Ignite Your Life and Fulfill Your Divine Purpose.* She does private readings, small group readings, or large-scale events.

I emailed Rebecca's website requesting an interview, not expecting to hear back. To my surprise, her assistant responded right away.

"We have to do this rather quickly as Rebecca is due at the end of May," her assistant wrote in an email.

"The sooner the better," I wrote. Within two days, the trip was arranged.

I was able to bring someone with me for the private reading and invited my friend Katie, one of my oldest friends since childhood, who lived in the Denver area. Katie and I both lost our fathers within a couple years of each other, and we had also both gone through a divorce at the same time. I figured a little wisdom from our dead dads might be just what the doctor ordered.

The night before our readings, Katie and I went to an Italian restaurant to get our thoughts together over meatballs and red wine.

"So how does this work?" Katie asked. "Do we ask questions or does she just tell us if there are dead people around?"

Katie was new to this medium stuff and didn't want to look like a rookie.

"I think it will be a little of both," I said. "She doesn't even know your name, so it will be interesting to see what comes up."

"By the way, we never got our salad," Katie said, realizing that the waiter had messed up our order.

Just then, the salad was put in front of us.

"Arugula for dessert?" I joked.

"We're still working out the kinks," the waiter said, "We just opened a couple of days ago. So sorry about that."

The next morning, Katie and I were chatting over coffee before hitting the road to Rebecca's office, and I was teasing her about the dead bananas on her counter.

"Are you saving these for banana bread?" I asked.

"I love making banana bread, but my stove is broken," she said.

She grabbed the bananas and tossed them in the garbage.

"Let's get going in case there is traffic," she said, grabbing her keys.

Rebecca's office was warm and welcoming. Katie and I were greeted by the staff and sat on the comfy couch as Rebecca finished up with a phone reading. Within a few minutes, it was our turn.

"Welcome!" Rebecca said, with a beaming smile, giving us hugs.

You know how some pregnant women just ooze that glow of "I'm so happy, I could burst"? Well, that was Rebecca, times ten. I had had a miserable pregnancy, yet somehow, this woman made me wish I had a bun in the oven.

She's so adorable!

Katie and I sat down as Rebecca explained how the session would work.

"So, I always say the work speaks for itself," she said, getting comfortable. "There's going to be things that come up there is no way I could know. And you know that."

"By the way, when are you due?" Katie asked.

"May 24," she said, putting her hands on her belly. "I got remarried to my husband Chris, and we have five kids between us. This was really unexpected, but we are so excited."

"Congratulations," I said.

"Thank you!" she said. "Okay, so now, here's what happens. I'm going to say a silent prayer to protect us, and then I'm going to have both of you say your first names. And then I'll tell you who's there, give validation, guidance, whatever you need. I do that for as long as it's flooding me, and then at the end, for the last ten minutes, I see if you have any questions. So we'll see what happens."

Rebecca closed her eyes and was silent for about fifteen seconds, we each said our first names, and then, "Okay, have both of your dads passed away?"

"Yes," I said.

"All I know is they are buddies," she said. "And one is Tom, or T as in Tom. Is that your dad?" she asked pointing to me.

"Tim was my dad," I said.

"Tim, it's for you," she said, pointing to me. "He's a character. He's fun and he's strong, and he wants me to tell you he's been behind the scenes for a long time. So he died a while ago?"

"About fifteen years," I said.

"Okay, he really gets what this is all about," she said. "He wished he would have understood this before he died. That just means that once he got up there he was pleasantly surprised to see that there was more. You've always known. You have a son?"

"Yes," I said.

"Something about him being your teacher," she continued. "Dad is so proud of you. And did you divorce? That was good. There was something about standing your ground and speaking your truth and not giving your power away . . . I don't know who the C is, is the C an ex-husband?"

"Yes," I said.

"Your dad is your son's guide," she said. "He knows him on a soul level. He comes to him when he's sleeping, so it's almost like at night your son gets the connection or clair-cognizance. It's like he just wakes up knowing stuff. Nurture that."

Rebecca kept her eyes closed for a few seconds and then opened them to bring Katie's dad into the picture.

"Okay, he is so happy, strong, back to his old self," Rebecca said. "Picture him being twenty-year-old some-thing. He's the same way her dad was [pointing to me], relieved there is truth to all of this. . . . Does your mom come from a very religious side? Catholicism?"

"Lutheran," Katie said. "Super Lutheran."

"What's going on is your dad is showing me many paths to one truth," she said. "He wants you to be spiritual, not necessarily religious. I don't know that your mom or her family understood this. But he's showing me whatever you're doing, keep doing it."

Katie had ditched her religious upbringing a long time ago to embrace yoga and hiking the mountains for her spiritual practice. It's been a much better fit.

"Was your dad a really likeable personality?" Rebecca asked, looking at me.

"Yes," I said.

"There's something about you and he are really alike," she said. "People are drawn to you and your real purpose is to be a networker and bringing people together . . . It's going to morph into something bigger and it feels like—have you ever thought about doing a TV show?"

"Yes," I said.

"You're going to do one," she said. "It's like you're the host of something. It's not yet. They show me 2017 as either when it happens or when you pitch it."

Works for me.

"Did you ladies just have Italian food? Your dads are showing me sitting with you at dinner. To be really specific, did one of your meals come out wrong?"

OMG!

"Yeah, they gave us the salad last," I said.

"They're laughing about that little glitch," she said. "That they were there. I think they did it to give you something to let you know they were sitting with you at dinner."

You can't Google that.

"Who is in New York City? Do you have family or friends there?" she asked, pointing to me. "They're talking about you going to visit and there's a reason you're going to visit."

"Yes, I'm gong in a few weeks for an interview with author and medium Concetta Bertoldi," I said.

"Who's David?" Rebecca asked, looking in my direction. "I keep hearing that. Do you know a David who was instrumental in your life?"

"That was my first love," I said. "When I was eighteen, nineteen."

"There's something going on with the pattern in your relationships," she said. "And it's all about—you've gotten everything else in your life under control and down, and this is your last big lesson. He wants you to get it right."

So do I!

"And it's something about not feeling that you're going to be abandoned or left behind and that you're going to have somebody strong enough to be your equal," she said.

Hello, Universe? I'd like to place an order for an equal. I'll have that "for here" please.

"Dad just showed me taking David, and your ex-husband, and all these people and creating this mold of all of their positive qualities into this final package. Forty-six. Are you forty-six?" she asked.

"I'll be forty-six in the fall," I said.

"Forty-six is your year that it happens, so don't be afraid to let it in," she said.

Noted!

"Your seventeen-year-old—is he really smart?" she asked, pointing to Katie who had two sons, ages seventeen and fifteen.

"He's intense and a perfectionist," Katie said.

"He is one of your teachers about patience," she said. "Something about not reacting to him. Keeping your cool. You are married, true?"

"I'm divorced," Katie said.

"They're showing me your kids' dad and you being married to him," she said.

"I'm actually, you know what though, I'm legally separated, so I guess I am still married," Katie said, kind of flustered.

I had no idea Katie was still legally married.

"The other son is the total opposite. I don't know if it's because he's really laid back. Is he the more social of the two? They're showing me the social butterfly, so you've kind of got a yin and yang between the two," Rebecca said.

"Yes, that's so true," Katie said.

"Were you not there when your dad died?" Rebecca asked Katie.

"No," Katie said.

"You weren't supposed to be," Rebecca said. "I don't know if on some level you feel sad or guilty about some of that, but he's showing me he visited you after he left his body. You weren't supposed to physically do more or say more."

"That's very nice to know," Katie said, holding back tears.

Rebecca then talked about how Katie's grandmother, who was cold as ice, wished she'd done a better job of being nurturing and how Katie's sons are teachers to her ex as my son is a teacher to mine.

"Your dad really wants you to trust," Rebecca said, looking at me. "There's some lesson you're at right now. Not trying to force or control things, but to just *be*. Go with the flow."

All right, all right already!

"Are you allergic to bees?" she asked me.

"Yes," I said.

"Your dad is using a bee to get your attention. He may not sting you, but it's a reminder to 'just be.' It will be a real clear sign. I'm going to stop here. Do you have any questions?"

Katie and I looked at each other, not quite sure where to start.

"I was ready to surrender that maybe being in a relationship was not my destiny," I said. "I've had two broken hearts since my divorce, so I was all set to say my purpose is to just write and be with my son. Maybe being in a relationship is not my special purpose."

"You *are* supposed to be in one; it's just not with those men," Rebecca said. "I don't see that you missed the boat with anybody. I see all the people behind you had a purpose for a reason, a season, not a lifetime. Your dad is saying there's somebody else you have not met yet. He's very outdoorsy. They're showing me Lance Armstrong."

Minus the steroids, I hope.

"He probably likes to cycle. Do you bike?" she asked.

"I will start!" I said.

"Dad, what else do you want her to know?" Rebecca asked, looking up at the sky. "Somebody is going to give you a crystal, a rock. Somehow that's a sign from your dad. Do you know a guy named Joe who died? A young friend?"

"My friend Joe from college just gave me a heart-shaped crystal," I said. "He's alive, but he just gave it to me the other night."

That is so weird!

"That's your dad working through Joe," she said. "It's all about healing your heart. It's your dad's way of reminding you how strong you are and not to give your power away."

Rebecca then mentioned Katie's dad's nickname.

"What do you want her to know?" Rebecca asked the sky, referring to Katie's dad. "He just wants you to understand that everything played out the way it was supposed to be, but in some way you're feeling let down. I don't know if it's the men in your life have just really disappointed you and haven't been there for you?"

"That's for sure," Katie said

"Your dad is saying to you . . . you guys are so parallel in these lessons. It's a pattern, yes, but it wasn't necessarily anything you had to learn. You attracted all these people who have the same wounds or issues, so do not personalize it like 'What's wrong with me?' Take your power back and say, 'I'm done with that. I'm not taking care of someone. I am strong. I want an equal who is strong and who will give back to me as much as I give to him.'"

I want an equal who is strong and who will give back to me as much as I give to him.

"So set that intention, and the Universe will bring that around," she said. "You are not with this person right now. If you're dating someone, eh, it's fine. Don't . . . get . . . serious."

I was so relieved to hear this because I was not a fan of the guy Katie was "kind of" dating. My nickname for him was "50-Cent" because he was likely to cancel on her 50 percent of the time.

"It's time to be done with your marriage," Rebecca said to Katie. "Your kids are going to be fine. They'll be going through the normal kids' stuff but nothing traumatic that they can't deal with . . . Don't apologize to them for divorcing. This needs to happen. Your husband is—you can't trust him. Did he cheat on you? There's a lack of loyalty, and he can't even be true to himself. You need to be done."

So true!

"The rest of this year is all about taking care of you, and then it happens," Rebecca said to Katie.

"Also, who is Lulu?" she asked.

I couldn't believe my ears.

"That's my ex-husband's grandmother," I said. "But we never met."

"It doesn't matter, she's part of your ancestry and she is a big fan of yours," she said. "She sends her love. And who is M? Mary? I know that's a common name, but I'm getting Mary."

Neither of us could figure out who that is.

"Or Ed? Charles?"

Nope.

"This could be for my next reading, too," she said. "That happens a lot. There is no time and space on the other side, and so this might be for somebody else. But ask your family, just in case."

Rebecca then had Katie's dad back in the picture.

"Do you make banana bread?" she asked Katie.

Seriously!?

"I do, and I just threw away a pile of bananas!" Katie said with a laugh.

"Your dad is showing me, 'Make banana bread' and he's smiling about that, so he was with you. He wants you to know that," she said.

On the drive home, Katie and I deconstructed our reading. She called her mother and asked about Mary, Ed, and Charles. None of them rang a bell. As for the things that stuck, while some of what came up could obviously be researched, you can't ask Siri *"Show me what kind of restaurant Jen and Katie went to last night where the waiter screwed up the order."*

"Now I need to get my stove fixed so I can make banana bread," Katie joked.

A dead dad talking about making banana bread surely isn't telling you the winning lottery numbers, but it was pretty mind-blowing.

The next morning, I went back to Rebecca's so I could sit in on one of her spirit circles. There were eight people in her office, five women and three men. They had all paid several hundred dollars to be there and traveled quite a distance, ranging from Montreal to Chicago.

Each of them had some sort of loss, most of them tragic, from dead kids to relatives who had committed suicide. I sat at a table in the back to observe and record the two-hour event.

"Whatever brought you here, your spirit guides, angels, and dead loved ones—could be all of them—but know that I don't bring through dark, fearful energy," Rebecca said, addressing the crowd. "Set your intention for who you want to hear from and what you want to know and then let it go and trust you will get what you need."

Rebecca reached down to her recording device.

"I record these sessions—this is very important. Very often I give people information that they just don't know. We could sit here all day, and we just won't figure it out. You have to go home and ask somebody else . . . I'm pretty good at telling if you're trying to force a fit, too. Also, there's a reason you are here in this group—it happens in every group—where some of the messages will be parallel. If you have an emotional response to someone else's reading, that is your spirit up there saying, 'Pay attention.' They brought you into this group and not last week's group. You may have similar challenges or losses. Listen and know your dead people all know each other. Once we die, they are all connected. They are helping each other."

Rebecca then walked the group through a meditation and started getting messages.

"Mary," she said right off the bat. "I have Mary here."

Two women raised their hands to say their mother's name was Mary.

"This is funny, because yesterday we had a Mary, do you remember?" Rebecca said, looking at me with a smile. "Yesterday Mary would not go away, and we couldn't make it fit. Last night I kept hearing Mary when I was on the couch. So in this meditation, Mary came back to me."

The Mary moms gave messages to their kids and sent birthday greetings and career validations. She then started talking to a man who owns a salon about his would-be father-in-law. After giving him a message, she said, "Okay, there's a Richard who died. I've heard it three times now. Does anybody know who Richard is?"

Richard was the name of my ex-husband's father. He died when his son and I were dating.

"It could be for anybody in this room," Rebecca said, looking right at me.

"That was the name of my ex-father-in-law," I said.

"He's up here trying to be recognized," she said, looking up at the corner of the room. "What is it that he wants us to know? He's sorry. *Huge* apologies. This man really screwed up. And he wants to help make it right from the other side. He's trying to help your living son to heal your ex-husband. There's a very strong karmic connection going on with your son and your ex."

Richard worked hard and provided for his family, but was never described as being "warm and fuzzy." Thankfully, my ex goes out of his way to be there for our son.

"And I don't know if April would have been a birth or death date?" She asked. "Mid-April?"

"My son's birthday is April 14," I said.

"He's really trying to be a guide for your son," she said. "That's why he's around."

Rebecca then turned to a woman who was slouched over in her chair, her face dripping with grief. She apparently had had a two-year-old son who drowned and a husband who was killed in a car wreck. The fact that she could get out of bed at all was miraculous to me.

"What did you just do to your hair?" Rebecca asked.

"I colored it for the trip," she said through her tears.

"Your son likes it. He shows me roses, which means, 'I love you,'" she said, as the woman wept harder. "He is with his father. Your son helped him to cross over and is showing him the ropes. Your husband is so sorry. 'Dad is okay, but he has a lot of work to do'—this is your son talking. Your husband is owning his death in some way . . . Did you get a tattoo for your son on your foot? He loves it . . . Do you have a ladybug connection? What is it?"

"That's the tattoo I got for my son," she said.

Holy moly!

"Your daughters need you, so this is all about helping you heal so you can be there for them," she said. Not only did this woman have a dead child and husband, but two small daughters under the age of five. "Is there a joke about green beans?"

"I always make them," she said.

"Your husband is teasing about the green beans," she said. "He wants you to make peace with his death because you keep replaying it over and over. He wants you to remember him happy. He doesn't want you to remember him in the body bag."

The woman let out a huge sob, and I watched as her shoulders moved up and down. I wanted to walk over to her and hold her in my arms until she needed to be let go.

There were many parallels in the group, from career paths to similar ways the loved ones crossed over. Out of the entire two hours, the most impressive reading to me was of the mother with the ladybug tattoo.

"Anyone who came through today, you have access to," Rebecca said to the room as she was finishing up. "You don't need me or another medium to do this. Everyone has their own direct line if you choose to meet them halfway. You showed up today, so you met them halfway. So when you go home, keep that door open, and in the next few days or weeks you may have extra vivid dreams, strong feelings, signs. Spirits only come to us if they think they've got our attention . . . So keep the door open and help this to be a 'to be continued.'"

As the room was clearing out, I went up to the woman with the ladybug tattoo. Her name was Jenny.

"Did you travel far to get here?" I asked.

"I came from Sacramento," said Jenny, who shared that she was a hairdresser. "I saved up for a while to do this. I was really hesitant to do a group because I didn't want to be so emotional in front of strangers."

"Are you glad you did it?" I asked.

Jenny's eyes welled up even more as she blotted them with a tissue.

"I really needed some comfort, because I've just been so . . . uncomfortable," she said, still crying.

A couple of the others came up to Jenny and shared that they, too, had lost a child to drowning—another parallel the group had in common. They walked out together, forever changed by the messages they had received over the last two hours.

After everyone had gone, Rebecca and I sat down for a follow-up conversation.

"How do your kids and stepchildren cope with what you do for a living?" I asked.

"I think I'm really blessed in that I'm in a time in life where it's much more accepted and talked about versus when I started it twenty years ago," she said. "And so it hasn't really been an issue with my kids. It's almost as though they don't know any differently. It's what mom does. And because I get very little push back, I'm very blessed. And the reason I think I'm supported in this is because I'm kind of the girl next door. I'm like everybody else. I'm not immune to life's challenges. And I always say the work speaks for itself. People can make up their mind or judge, but I say, 'Just watch,' and then usually they're speechless."

"So for people who will say you're Googling everyone you have in a circle, what do you say?" I asked.

"How could I know about the ladybug tattoo?"

Exactly.

"That's why I don't argue with skeptics at all," she said. "It just gets me frustrated."

"What do you say to the religious folks who feel this goes against the Bible?" I asked.

"The bottom line is, do these people pray to Jesus? Then they're talking to the dead, too," she said.

Snap!

"We are all in some way, shape, or form connecting to spirit when we pray," she continued. "I'm not going to the dead, they are coming to me, and I'm choosing to answer the call. I have a brother who is a rabbi. . . . He wrote this whole thing about this—how mediumship goes back centuries. I've had a lot of rabbis say, 'It's the intention behind it that matters.' My intention is for healing and for light. My intention is for good."

"Do you think there is such a thing as an 'oops' death?" I asked.

"Yes, suicide is sometimes this," she said. "There's a difference between an accident and a suicide. But when the spirit owns it, they're basically taking responsibility for their choices that led to their death, and the 'oops' would be, 'I didn't intentionally set out to overdose, but I did. And had I made different choices, I might have been here another ten years.'"

"Is it possible for someone to hide their secrets from a medium or psychic, because I seem to attract people who like to keep secrets," I said, thinking of the last couple of guys I dated.

"Yes, so when I read somebody, I can only read what they are willing to share," she said. "Before we go on, can I just share the hit I'm getting on you?"

Uh, yeah!

"The reason you attract those people is because you are committed to transparency and truth, right? So you are bringing to you people who are the contrast of that, and you're giving them the opportunity to be transparent and truthful," she said. "Whether or not they choose to rise up and be that is another story. You're not responsible for that. So if you're wondering 'Why do I keep attracting this?' On some level they want that and need that to heal. I think this validates you—that you're doing nothing wrong."

Amen, sister!

"You predict things for people when you give them readings, but with free will, anyone can change their path at any moment," I said. "So do you believe in destiny?"

"I believe we come in with these loose scripts, like it's a predestined path but free will absolutely plays a part in whether or not that unfolds," she said. "So when I do readings, the guidance on the future is always loosely based on the choices you're making, and if you continue to go with the flow and make those choices, probably this is going to happen. But at any point you can interfere and change the outcome. I just tell people to pray for their highest truth to come along."

"What are your feelings about karma?" I asked. "I got stuck in the snow in my car last winter, and it was so frustrating, I started to wonder if it was some karma where I had buried someone in the snow in a past life or something."

"Are there karmic debts? Yes," she said. "Maybe you put out negative energy or lack of compassion to a friend who recently went through a car issue, and so you had to deal with a car issue to be humbled. I totally believe the Universe has a way of balancing itself out. Everything you put out there is a boomerang. It comes back. So you might as well be intentional in what you put out there."

"What's one thing you want readers of this book to remember on a daily basis based on all the knowledge you've gathered over the years?" I asked.

"Accountability—that everything you say, think, and do follows you. I hear this all the time from the spirits: they didn't realize how powerful they were and that everything follows you. You pick up where you left off. You're not being judged when you go to the other side, but you take a self-inquiry and inventory with your panel of guides and you have to own all of it. As a human being, sometimes I'm exhausted at the end of the day and I get short with my kids and I get reactive because I'm in fear, and before I react, I stop and I say, 'Please align my thoughts and energy now with God and with love.' You have to choose to come from love. Because again, everything you put out there comes back to you, whether it's right away or down the road, little or big, it does."

A few days after my trip to see Rebecca, I was shopping in an antiques store when I was struck by several images on a table in the corner. I noticed a large bumblebee and various tiles with different words or phrases including "Bee Happy," "Bee My Baby," "Family," "Apple of my eye," and finally "Jen."

I thought of the words of Rebecca from my personal reading: "Your dad really wants you to trust. There's some lesson you're at right now. Not trying to force or control things. But to just *be*. Go with the flow. Your dad is using a bee to get your attention. He may not sting you, but it's a reminder to 'just be.' It will be a real clear sign."

That's weird.

5

Concetta Bertoldi

WHEN CONCETTA BERTOLDI WAS GROWING UP in Montville, New Jersey, in the 1960s and '70s, she knew she was different from other kids in her small, rural town. From a very early age, she would get intuitive hits about things she couldn't possibly know.

One night when Concetta was sixteen, she woke up to the sight of several dead people singing songs and having a party in her bedroom. She screamed for her parents in a total panic, and while neither her mother nor her father shared the ability to see ghosts, Concetta's paternal grandfather had been a medium, so the subject matter wasn't totally foreign to the family.

"These spirits simply want your help," her father told her, drawing from the little experience he had growing up with a dad who saw dead people.

"I don't want to help them!" Concetta said, thinking about her new boyfriend Tony and how she wanted to be a normal teenager who wore lipstick and went to school dances.

"If you really feel that way, say 'In the name of God, please go!' and they will leave you alone," her father said. "But you really have to be sure you want them to leave before you say that."

Concetta weighed her options and decided boys and makeup sounded more appealing than a dead-people dance party. She chanted, "In the name of God, please go" as many times as she could muster, and to her surprise, the ghosts took their show on the road.

When she got into her twenties, her abilities slowly started to resurface, but Concetta still kept things on the down low. Even her husband, John, was shielded from the news for fear he'd run screaming from the room if he knew the whole story.

It wasn't until her brother Harold died from AIDS in 1991 that she decided to go public.

"People need these messages," Harold told her from the other side. "We will help you."

Now living in Boonton, New Jersey, with John (her husband of thirty-two years, who thankfully hasn't been scared away by his wife's job), Concetta has a seven-year waiting list for her private reading sessions and several best-selling books, including *Do Dead People Watch You Shower?* and *Do Dead People Walk Their Dogs?*

I met Concetta on a warm spring day in New Jersey where she was doing a live event for about two hundred people at the Holiday Inn in Totowa.

"Hi, darling!!" she screamed, hugging me (I mean, REALLY hugging me) at first sight in the lobby.

Concetta wore a blue and white top and had bright red lips and a smile that could charm the pants off of even my dead, crabby grandpa. Her eyes sparkled when she talked, and speaking of talking, I'd never met a person with a stronger New Jersey accent.

"We have seats blocked out for youze," she said, holding my shoulders. "Oh, my *Gawwwd*, you are *adaaahrable!*"

While some strong New Jersey accents can make people less attractive (think Snooki from *Jersey Shore*), Concetta's made her more *adaahrable,* which I didn't think was possible since I already wanted to kidnap and hide her in my roll-on luggage.

I looked around the lobby to size up the crowd. There seemed to be just as many men as there were women, and the ages ranged from eight years young to eighty-five years old. The feeling in the room was a combination of anticipation and overwhelming grief. Many people held tissues and would cry with no warning.

One woman sitting across from me had such a pained look on her face, my mind was racing as I wondered what horrible act she had witnessed or survived.

"I am going to weep just looking at these people," I said to my friend Peter, who was my "anonymous plus one" for the event.

As I settled into my seat near the front, I started chatting with the woman next to me, who said her name was Pamela. She seemed to be about fifty and was with one of her girlfriends.

"Have you been to something like this before?" I asked her.

"Oh, I've been to a ton of her events," Pamela said. "Concetta is the real deal."

"Have you seen other mediums?" I asked.

"Absolutely," she said. "I lost my son David to a brain tumor twenty-one years ago. He was only seven. I remember going to see medium John Edward back when he was working out of his house, charging just seventy-five bucks a session."

I know how hard it had been coping with a father who died from a brain tumor at the age of fifty-six. I couldn't imagine being a mother and losing a son to the same fate at the tender age of seven.

"I'm so sorry for your loss," I said. "I hope he comes to you today with a message."

"So do I," Pamela said, her expression getting more serious.

Hey, Dad, if you're up there, can you go find David and tell him to start blabbing in Concetta's ear? He might be shy, and you're a professional at this stuff, so go do what you can, okay?

Soon after 11 a.m., Concetta made her way out to greet the room.

"We have spent time praying for you before we got started, and we have so many dead folks here today," Concetta said walking from one side of the room to the other. "If you think THIS room is crowded, if you saw all the dead folks, you'd be blown away! My hope is that you all see this evidence by the souls that come through, that it is true and we really don't die."

Concetta then explained that sometimes the spirits will guide her to their loved ones by standing over them or near them, even waving if necessary. Other times, she might feel an urge to speak to someone, and then she will ask that person to say the name of the spirit they hope to contact to cut to the chase.

"I want to get to as many people as possible today," she said. "Now I want to share a story with you. So many times people will ask me if something is a coincidence. My friend Leanna who works with us, her father passed away about five months ago, and her sister's birthday was this month. Her son came in the house from the mailbox and said, 'Mommy, it's a card.' And the boy had a shocked look on his face and she said, 'What's the matter?' and he said, 'This card is from Grandpa.' It was a birthday card that he had written to his daughter a year ago postmarked from 2015 that never got to her. It got there on the day of her birthday in 2016! They all said, 'Can you ask Concetta if that is a coincidence?' I said, 'Do you really need me to tell you? No, your father made sure that card got to you.' What are the odds? He made that happen. So you see, they are with us. They are always within reach."

Concetta then made her way to a woman in the front row.

"What is your name, sweetheart?" Concetta asked.

"Linda Gonzales, and I'm looking for my son," she said, wiping a tear.

"Before I ask you about your son, who is the A, or Al? Alice?" Concetta asked.

"That's my mother," Linda said.

"She's saying, 'Tell her Al sends her love,'" Concetta said. "She says, 'Tell her I have the boy with me.' He is at great peace. He's messed with the lights, and he knows that you know. "

Linda gasped as she covered her mouth with her tissue.

"Is he okay?" Linda asked through a sob.

"Oh, honey, we're the ones in the tough spot," Concetta said. "This is camp Earth. This is not an easy place to be! Where we're going to from here is home. This is only just a mirage, basically. And we are so consumed with material things and physical things that we get distracted from where we really came from. So trust and believe that we don't die and your son is in a miracle of a place. He wants you to remember always and he remembers how much you love him. And remember that your grief is always as deep as your love."

Your grief is always as deep as your love.

"You have to go through life knowing that someday you will be reunited with him, but do the best you can now and be happy because that's what he wants for you," Concetta continued. "So stop wishing you were with him, because he is saying you have to be there for the others. It's not your time. He knows you wish you could be with him. He'll see you again because the best is yet to come. That's a promise from God, and I just like saying it! I'm so sorry, darling. Sorry for all these losses."

Concetta put her hand on the woman's knee as she wept silently into her tissue.

"Thank you," Linda said, wiping her face.

Out of all the mediums I've seen in action, Concetta was by far the most empathetic. If she had had enough time to hug every person in the room, she would have done so happily.

"I'd like to go to the back row," Concetta said, pointing to a young man in his twenties. "What is your name, honey?"

"My name is Christian, and I'm looking for my grandfather," he said.

"I've got him right here," Concetta said with a huge grin. "He's talking about New Year's Eve parties and shows me all the corny decorations. And he loved it all and the music and the dancing," she added, as the whole row laughed with confirmation. "When he passed away, he was in the hospital and not everyone could get there, and he knows that and that you feel terrible about that, Christian. He knows that it was really heartbreaking for you because that was your biggest thing was to say, 'goodbye,' and to get there."

Christian started sobbing uncontrollably as the woman next to him (who may have been his mother) tried to comfort him by rubbing his back.

"Please know, sweetie, that it doesn't matter and that he wants you to remember the life he had with you and not the last moments of his life," Concetta said. "So please understand that he knows that's a heartbreak for you. And he's trying to take it away from you. You were his first grandchild, and he was so proud when they put you in his arms. He's showing me a photograph of himself holding you as a baby, and you were the first one."

Christian and the woman next to him both let out a big cry.

"You made him prouder than anything, and know that he is young and gorgeous and handsome where he is," she said. "All the pain and that sick body is gone. And he can hear you, and so when you need him, you need to only talk to him, and he will help you. Just bring God into it. Say, 'In the name of God, hear my prayer,' and you will be okay. He does want you to get rid of that guilt of not being there at the hospital because there is no need for that. He wanted to be released because he was suffering and he wanted to go home. He says, 'I love you, I love you, I love you.' If I could get to the back row, I would give you such a hug, you sweetie pie."

The crowd clapped as Concetta moved to another part of the room. She stopped in front of a sweet man with white hair.

"What's your name and who are you looking for, honey?" she asked the man.

"My name is Alan, and I'm looking for my wife Eve," he said.

Concetta stopped cold in her tracks.

"Oh, I got her right away," she said. "She's sitting right next to you. She is loving you big-time, Al!"

Even though this event was sold out, the seat next to Alan was mysteriously unoccupied.

"She actually made sure nobody took that seat so she could be next to you," Concetta continued as the room laughed. "She *adores* you. Oh, the two-a-youze are just so cute! She's showing me a yearbook. Were you high school sweethearts?" Alan nods "yes." "Oh, my Gawwwd, Al, this woman adores you, honey. She says, 'I'm sorry I had to go home. I wouldn't have left you if I didn't have to.' She knows you've held everything down in your gut. You're so worried about everyone else's feelings. She's worried about your stomach. It's all your stress, my darling, because you don't want to talk about it. And she wants you to know that you talk to her about it when you're alone. You have long conversations with her in the bedroom. She shows you walking around the bedroom and in the closet and the bathroom. It wasn't the kitchen or living room; it was the bedroom for you two."

Alan nodded "yes" while wiping away a tear.

"Tell my husband he was the best husband and the best friend and 'I adore you', she says. 'I love you forever and always.' You are going to be here a long time, Al, so don't go wishing you could be with her. I know everybody wonders 'When can I get the next ticket out of here?' She says, 'My love, we'll be together again.' She wants you to know that she can remember everything where she is now, because at the end her mind was forgetting things and that was very upsetting for her. She says, 'I have it all back. I love you.'"

Alan looked exactly like the "best husband and best friend" anyone could ask for. He hung on to every word that came out of Concetta's mouth.

I wonder if Al and Eve have a single son?

For the next two and a half hours, Concetta moved through the room bringing through children, parents, grandparents, aunts, uncles, and siblings whose deaths were as varied as cancers, HIV, suicides, car accidents, and heart attacks. Sometimes she pulled names out of thin air, and other times, the names didn't even come up, just the specific way the person went to the other side. One spirit was even making fun of the family for putting so many "doodads" in the casket when he was buried. And then there was the grandmother who wanted her granddaughter to be more discerning with her choice in men.

"You MUST choose wisely because you have chosen some real mammalukes," Concetta said, causing the woman and her entire family to laugh. "That's Italian slang, but it means those guys were not good enough for you. She's saying, 'You get the right guy!' and she says she told you this ALL THE TIME. She was very protective of you, and she says you are the cat's meow. So just say this, 'In the name of God, hear my prayer.' Because your grandmother is one with God, so ask her for help. They don't get bored with our asking them."

"She is really impressive," Peter whispered in my ear.

"Indeed," I said, looking at the woman next to me who'd lost her son.

Please bring through the seven-year-old.

Concetta walked over in our direction and stopped suddenly as she got in front of my new friend Pamela.

"Forgive me, but you have a child who passed away," Concetta said.

"Yes, I do," Pamela said.

Thank God!

"Right here is the child," she said. "He's a boy child, maybe seven or eight, and he loves his mother very much. He's telling me, 'Send my love to my mother. I'm right here.' He has siblings he adores. I don't know what is going on in your life, but it seems like a whirlwind right now. It seems like you're trying to go from here to there to there to here, and you can't get there fast enough . . . But he's sure you can do it. He's telling me, 'You're going to be happy. You finally find happiness.' Your 2020, 21, 22 are the best years coming up for you. I have no idea what's going on there, but that's what he's showing me. In all fairness to you, there are babies being born to you. You're in for a wonderful time."

Pamela and her friend both smiled and cried silently.

"He so wants you to know that he has helped you along, especially with his siblings. He has a brother that talks about him all the time. Looks like there are one, two, three, four, how many children? Five? Wow, you look great. Gawwwd bless you! Who is David?"

"My son who died," Pamela said, her voice cracking.

"He loves you so much, darling, and you're in good health so don't you worry," Concetta said. "He wants you to tell his siblings and his father that he loves them. God bless you, honey. I'm so sorry for your loss."

Well done, David!

Concetta put her hand on Pamela's knee as she and her friend shared an "Oh My God" glance before Concetta was on to the next dead person.

"Who are you looking for?" Concetta said approaching my friend Peter.

"My dad William—alias 'Big Bill,'" Peter said.

"Let me ask you something, because he's really cute, your dad, but do you look more like your mother than your dad?" Concetta asked.

"Yes," Peter said.

"He says, 'This is my son, but with my wife's face.' He says he loved your mother and he loves you. Did your father smoke?"

"Yes," Peter said.

"God, he's making me smell it," Concetta said. "He's saying, 'Don't let any of the kids smoke. Don't smoke.' I smell the smoke. It had something to do with his crossing. He's talking about many years where people told him, 'Don't smoke anymore,' and he didn't listen. He just said, 'Yeah, yeah,' but he still did it. Did he tell you in confidence some stories that you never betrayed him? Because he's saying, 'Thank you.' The things he told you were 'guy to guy' things, and he's so happy you were his son and that he could trust you. There were things he confided in with you about his youth and his childhood—many that if they wrote books about it now it may be a best seller because it was kind of comical. He was a riot! I can tell by his energy. He had a lot of stories to tell. Here is the good news, though: You're very healthy. You have a long life. He loves the way you take care of yourself."

This was welcome news, as Peter had just been given a clean bill of health after beating prostate cancer. Since his diagnosis, he had made many life changes to keep himself healthy.

"It seems as though next month there is a birthday. Who has the May birthday?" Concetta asked.

"That's my sister," Peter said.

"He said, 'Happy Birthday to her. Tell my other child happy birthday from Dad.' Hope this helps you," Concetta said.

I looked at Peter, who gave me a nod with a smile, indicating Concetta's reading was spot-on.

She then gave a message to a woman whose husband had died of cancer.

"Is he out of pain?" the woman asked, wiping her nose as she cried.

"He is no longer sick," Concetta said. "You must trust this. I saw my brother die at thirty-eight years old. He had AIDS. He looked like he was 180 years old, and he was only eighty pounds in that bed. When I see and hear my brother now, you would not believe how happy he looks. There is a place beyond here where we are as young and beautiful as we choose. So please know that."

The crowd clapped.

"You guys are so kind, I don't want youze to ever go home!" she said.

When Concetta finally finished (she ran nearly thirty minutes long), I leaned over to Pamela.

"How do you feel?" I asked.

"Peaceful," she said. "As much as I know that he's in a better place, it's like a phone call to my son. It's that reassurance that he's still in my life and knows what's going on and shares everything with us. It gives me chills. It's hard to describe, but it's a sense of peace and contentment, knowing that I'm going to see him again and that he's okay. And I'm in touch with him."

"Was Concetta right about you having a lot going on?" I asked.

"Your life is in a whirlwind right now," Pamela's friend said. "We were just talking about that on the way here."

"Do you have a son who talks about him more than the other children?" I asked.

"Mark, he was two years younger than David, and he kind of lost his role model," Pamela said. "He wants to believe in this, but he always asks, 'Do you think David is here?' I can't wait to tell him what happened today."

✠ ✠ ✠

After the event, Peter and I met Concetta and John for dinner, along with my friend Sal and his wife Chris.

"You like Italian?" John asked Sal as we got settled into our table.

"I *am* Italian," Sal said.

"Good, so am I," John said. "Concetta is half Sicilian and half Irish, so I say 'You gotta be careful because she'll kill you in your sleep with a potato!'"

John grew up in New Jersey, works in construction, and seemed to be the kind of guy who keeps his friends close and his enemies closer. If he liked you, you knew it. If he didn't like you, you REALLY knew it.

"I love their pesto here," Concetta said, looking at the menu. "Although John makes the best pesto."

"So you're good looking, and you cook, too, John?" I asked.

"You better believe it!" he said, cracking a smile.

"My mother was raised in an orphanage, so I was never taught to cook because *she* was never taught to cook," Concetta said. "John does all the cooking, and he's great at it! I used to be a little thin thing when we met, but now, I've put a little on. But I don't care because he likes me this way. I can still rock it and roll it around so who cares, you know what I mean?"

Within minutes, the first bottle of wine was history.

"Would you like a splash?" I asked Concetta, reaching for her glass.

"Oh, I don't drink, honey," Concetta said. "Could you imagine me on alcohol?! NOT a good thing."

"You are such a wonderful personality," I said. "Why don't you have your own reality show?"

"I did have some things I was working on in TV and got screwed over by a couple of producers because I trusted the wrong people," Concetta said. "It was very unfortunate. But I swear like a sailor, and I worried that people would think it lessens my abilities, but I like to say, 'That's just flair.'"

Note to television producers everywhere: Concetta Bertoldi would be television *GOLD!*

"Do you believe in karma?" I asked. "Maybe you had a past life with that producer or something?"

"I do believe hugely in karma, and I do think that everyone we've met before, we meet again," Concetta said.

"And sometimes there's unfinished business or there's recollection of something that was loving and beautiful at one time, or there was something that makes you put your dukes up. My mother in law, for example, hates my guts. It's so sad. From the first day I met her—I was twenty-eight years old—and the minute I met her, I went 'Oh!!' And I felt so bad because I really wanted to be liked. I never retaliated over the horrible things that she said or did. I always tried to keep the peace. Then in 2008, I wrote my first book, and I called her 'a rock in my underwear' and 'a real pickle puss.' *Well!* She finally had something she could hang her hat on. John has no relationship with her now either. It's sad. I didn't know the book was going to be a best seller and translated into fourteen languages! So now people in Japan know she's a pickle-puss and a rock in my underwear. Oh well!"

"Is she still alive?" Sal asked.

"Now she's ninety-four, and she flies over my house on a broom on a regular basis," Concetta said, as Sal almost spat out his wine with laughter. "That's the only time I see her, on Halloween or on my birthday when she's throwing darts."

"So do you think you had a past life together with *her?*" I asked.

"Oh, yes," Concetta said. "And what scares me, Jen, is the *next* life. I picture us at the table with my sweet Lord and him going, 'Concetta. Margaret. Girls . . . the next time you're going to be *sisters.*' And I'm gonna be like, 'OH, SHIT!'"

This was quickly becoming one of the most memorable dinners I'd had in years.

Great conversation? Check. Delicious food? Check. Hilarious medium? Check.

"So tell us, do the dead really watch us in the shower?" I asked. "I know the answer because I've read your books, but I'd love you to share your thoughts with the others."

"Sure they do, but they don't care," Concetta said. "I mean they're dead, so what are they gonna do?! But there is no room for judgment over there because it's all about love and forgiveness. They don't care if we have sex or what we do in the bathroom."

"*They* might not care, but I wouldn't want to see you guys in the shower," John said pointing to Sal and Peter.

The main course arrived, and everyone started passing around the plates.

"So in all the work you've done, what are your beliefs about Jesus?" Peter asked while grabbing some food. "Was he the son of God?"

"Absolutely," Concetta said.

"Everyone is though," said John, the Buddhist of the group.

"That's true," Peter said.

"I believe there are many hierarchy spirit masters, hierarchy mission entities, and hierarchy angels," Concetta said. "I believe he was a very evolved, highly evolved mission entity spirit master who came on earth and changed the world. And here's what we need to know: We see a lot of people like that, different variations of it, maybe something as simple as Michael Jackson or Marilyn Monroe—we are always going to remember these people. They are children of God. Maybe they didn't do the same things Jesus did, obviously, but they definitely qualify for coming here for a special mission from God, because we remember them around the world."

"That is one of the most beautiful things that came out of a session like today," Peter said. "That there is a God, and God loves us all."

"I always tell people we are here to love each other despite our differences," Concetta said. "That's it. If you think about it, there have been wars since the beginning of time over religion. Is this what God really wanted? No."

"I was raised Roman Catholic and I love the message, but there is no doubt that religion has messed up a really great message over time," Peter said.

"My mother was Catholic and my father was Protestant, and they said, 'We're not going to force our children to pick one or the other. We will let them grow up and decide for themselves,'" Concetta said. "My parents loved every religion that came in front of them. If they had a friend who was Jewish, they would celebrate Hanukkah."

"We should do that today," Peter said. "We should teach our children four or five different religions so they can get educated about what's out there."

"Yes, like being given the option of learning four or five languages," Concetta said. "So when I grew up with this ability and my parents said 'Choose which religion you want,' I didn't know where to go. But what I know now and what they tell me from the other side is that God is right *here*. Church is right *here*. My communication doesn't have to be a prayer out of a book. It has to come from my heart and my own soul. And then you've got religion. That's the way I live my life."

It has to come from my heart and my own soul. And then you've got religion.

"I have a problem with the whole 'If you don't love Jesus, you're going to hell,' piece," I said. "You mean to tell me if there is a child born in Africa who isn't a Christian, he will go to hell? Give me a break."

"My mother was raised in a Catholic orphanage," Concetta said. "She was raped, beaten, starved, and denied medical treatment every day of her life. Right here in New Jersey. She was there from ages three to eighteen. It was horrible for her. That kind of stuff makes me a little crazy. This place was supposed to protect her. So as a young girl, I identified religious people with keeping secrets and hurting my mother. So I had to recreate religion for myself and embrace God without having the anger that I did for what they did to my mother."

"The story of your mother's passing is incredible," I said, remembering it from her books.

"How did she pass?" Peter asked.

"When my mother was seven years old, she was supposed to have a visit with her mother on Thanksgiving Day," Concetta said. "Her mother was an alcoholic who couldn't care for her kids, but she was allowed visits. So on that Thanksgiving, my mother waited all day at the orphanage. She shivered at the end of the driveway in the cold, waiting for my grandmother to come and take her home, and her mother never came. The nun finally came out and said,

'Get inside. Your mother isn't coming. She's dead.' That's how they broke the news to a seven-year-old girl. My grandmother was just twenty-seven when she died. Seventy years later, my mother is in the hospital on Thanksgiving Day. She turns around and looks at my brother and said, 'Oh, my mother died on Thanksgiving.' Then she turned around and died. I said to my brother, 'Mommy's mommy kept her word. She came and took her daughter home on Thanksgiving Day seventy years later.' What are the odds?"

That's weird!

"Some mediums and psychics believe we choose our parents for the lessons, but I find that hard to believe when I hear about parents murdering their kids or making them become suicide bombers," I said.

"I was just seeing on the news the other day where some girl was being sent to jail for thirty-three years for setting her newborn on fire," Concetta said. "And then you look at someone like me who really wanted children and couldn't have them, so I'm like, 'What's up with this?!' But here's where I always get back to—I give my trust and faith to God, and I have to know that God has something in mind. These souls that come here and die so fast are making a sacrifice for all mankind and for something bigger than any of us can figure out. There's something bigger going on, otherwise, 'Why?'"

"Do you believe in life reviews?" Peter said.

"I absolutely do," Concetta said. "I do believe we are made to feel every single thing that we have put out there and made everybody feel. I also believe that immediately we are encouraged to forgive ourselves on the other side. But supposedly when we get to the other side, we are so aware of the divine spirit of God."

"Do you think every level is aware of the divine spirit of God?" Sal asked.

"No, I think there are many levels," Concetta said. "There are levels like there are schools here—grade school, middle school, high school, and college. The higher you go, the easier it is for you to forgive your soul."

"When the murderers cross over, do they feel sorry for what they did?" Sal asked.

"I have talked to many people I respect in my field about this," Concetta said. "I've asked what they hear, because I have my own thoughts on what I hear, but I've had an ongoing discussion with someone I really respect. She says when we get there, we are met with love. Even these people who commit these terrible crimes are forgiven by God. I'm like, 'What?!' I want to know there is retribution for whatever they've done. But I am coming at it in human form. It's hard for me to think as God would think because I'm not God."

"You said today that some people were going to get married or have children," I said. "What are your thoughts about free will versus what the spirits tell you about their loved ones' futures?"

"Not everybody is always going to have children or get married, but when people ask, 'Will I get married?' I don't want to say, 'No' because how do I know they won't put that into motion?" Concetta said. "I tell people what the spirits are telling me, and I'm a firm believer that you can put things into motion in your own life and you do that by opening up your mouth. So why not create the best scenario you can think of? Why not put it on a high level? I didn't go to college and I'm a *New York Times* best-selling author. How did that happen? I worked hard, did my best, put it into motion, prayed, and put my best out there."

Snap!

"What do you say to the skeptics?" I asked.

"Sometimes, people will walk in after being on the waiting list for years, and they'll say, 'I want the keys to the safe or the lottery numbers, otherwise I don't believe it's real.' And you know what I say to them? If they are rude like that, I say, 'I don't need your money and let's not do this.' I send them on their way and cut my losses."

"I do these live interview events with authors, and many have been mediums and psychics," I said. "I will get emails from people saying, 'Shame on you for being swindled. You call yourself a journalist? You're an idiot.' It's exhausting."

"And those people will never get the healing that is being handed to them," Concetta said. "You can't heal your grief if you are not open to this being real. It's just not possible."

You can't heal your grief if you are not open to this being real.

The check came and after a lot of arm wrestling between Sal and John, John came away victorious.

"Next time when you invite us to YOUR neck of the woods, you can pay, Sal," John said. "But I'll be expecting you to take us to a much nicer restaurant!"

Concetta then leaned in to me as if she was sharing a secret.

"Honey, you look just like your dad," she said.

I was wondering if he was going to show up.

"Many say we do share the same smile," I said. "It's not like my dad to miss a great Italian dinner, so I'm glad to know he made it to the party."

"He had a good vocabulary. A lot under the cap," Concetta said.

My father graduated from Yale and studied history, so I'd say that was pretty accurate.

"I got him, he's right here," she said looking to my right. "Who's name does he have? He has the same name as someone?"

"Well he was technically John Timothy, named after his father," I said.

"Your little sister, she is moving soon," she said.

"Yes, she is moving in just a few weeks," I said.

"And YOU—you're going to do great. And the people who know you, I mean *really* know you, love you. The ones you really trust. Your word is as good as gold. You don't have to worry about a freaking thing," Concetta said grabbing my arm.

No worrying? Then what am I going to do for the rest of my life?

"You're on the right track and doing what you're supposed to be doing, and the energy is all moving and shaking for you," she said, barely taking a breath because the message was coming so fast. "Nothing is stagnant and still. And remember—where you are working you need windows so energy is flowing. This is what keeps all the energies coming to you. It flows *through* you. And also, what they're telling me is that your last relationship, he had to go to make room for something else. Someone new is coming in and this is going to be the *wonderful* one, and there had to be space in between so you could appreciate it. Shit! It's going to be good, honey. Just trust."

There's that damn TRUST piece again.

"Oh, sweetie, I just want to tell you something," Concetta said, bringing her focus back to me and away from the area where my dead dad was standing. "I *adoooooore* you. I wish you lived around here because you would be my new best friend. You're one of the nicest ladies I have met in a long time. You're going to *have* to come back out here!"

Done and done!

"Wow, I gotta take off a layer," Concetta said, removing her sweater. "I think I'm having a hot flash."

"Honey?" Sal said, winking at his wife who had just made a similar statement.

"Somebody said to me once, 'What are you gonna say when you meet God, Concetta?' I said, 'Well, when I meet God, I'm going to ask him something that I feel all women would want to know. I really get the whole thing about being a woman and I've enjoyed it. The life changes that happened when I was a teenager, I get it. They had a purpose and a reason. But by the time you get to your fifties or earlier, they start to experience things that are called *menopause*. Does it have to include a hot flash every twenty minutes? I suggest a change and I'd like to fill out a form here to the hierarchy angels and ask them, 'Instead of having a hot flash every twenty minutes, I think we should have an orgasm every twenty minutes.' Wouldn't that be better? Just swap out the hot flash for an orgasm, and we'll be good."

"I'll drink to that," Chris said, raising her coffee cup.

Everyone raised their glass for a toast, which were mostly coffees and cappuccinos at this point since the wine was long gone.

"You've got to give me your card, John, so we can keep in touch," Sal said.

"I don't do cards," John said. "But I got a pen. You got a piece of paper?"

"You have to stay our friends now, honey, because you know too much!" Concetta said with a wink.

6

Paul Selig

"HAVE YOU THOUGHT ABOUT INCLUDING Paul Selig in your book?" Thomas John asked me one day after a show.

I like to think I'm pretty well versed in the metaphysical space, but I'd never heard of the guy.

"He's a channel," he continued.

In my world, a "channel" is something you tune in to for watching your favorite TV program. In Thomas's world, it's someone who communicates messages from other spirits or guides to either individuals or large groups.

"What he does is so different from, like, what I do or what a traditional medium does. So it would be good to include him," he said.

The next day I reached out to my publisher about putting Paul in the book. Within twenty-four hours, I received an email out of nowhere from my friend John St. Augustine, forwarding me a pitch he'd received from Paul Selig's publicist saying that Paul was coming in from New York to do an event in Chicago.

"This looks like a better fit for your podcast than for mine," he wrote.

I guess the Universe wants Paul in this book!

Raised an atheist in New York, Paul got his master's from Yale and served on the faculty of NYU and Goddard College. After a spiritual experience left him clairvoyant in 1987, he studied energy healing and discovered his unique ability to take on the physical characteristics of people that his clients inquire about during their readings. He then started channeling messages and tried to keep his gifts under wraps for years, even having an anonymous website so his friends in academia wouldn't know he was a "medium for the living." Known for channeling messages for hours at a time, when his eyes have reportedly changed color in the process, he has several best-selling books, including *I Am the Word*, *The Book of Love and Creation*, and *The Book of Knowing and Worth*. His works have gained him international notoriety and even celebrity endorsements from the likes of Sammy Hagar and Deepak Chopra.

His publicist sent me his latest book, *The Book of Mastery*, in which Paul's guides (at one point they say there are nine of them) share wisdom on everything from manifestation to surrendering to the unknown.

We arranged for an interview to take place at WGN studios for my podcast on a Friday before his weekend workshop in Chicago.

As I entered the lobby, I saw a tall man with a kind face and a white beard sitting on the bench.

"Are you Paul?" I asked.

"Yes," he said, rising to shake my hand.

Paul looked and sounded like the professor I wish I'd had in college. He had respect oozing from his pores, and his demeanor was purposeful and intense.

As we settled into our conversation in the studio, Paul revealed that he was not only a channel but also an empath and an intuitive.

"When I was twenty-five, I was about a year out of Yale graduate school, and I'd really hit a wall," he said. "I think I had a list of who I thought I was supposed to be, and I'd suddenly attained that list, and I wasn't okay with my list. I started looking for something more, really out of sheer necessity. . . . I actually heard a voice telling me to get my act together, which was the first thing that opened me, and then a few months later I had an experience with energy that left me seeing little lights around people. . . . And in that moment in my life, from having gone from a world where there was no God to one where maybe perhaps there was, I thought, 'If there is, why couldn't people just wake up?' I think in that moment there was an innocence attached to my framework of what could be. So I went up to my roof and tried to teach myself to meditate, and I asked to be woken up."

Paul then explained how he had felt a flood of energy move through his body unlike anything he'd experienced.

"I won't say that I became enlightened, because I don't consider myself to be enlightened," he continued. "But I think that for me and who I was at that time in my life, I needed something that was tangible for me to go on this journey with, and I was given that. I'm not a very good 'new ager.' I'm skeptical about a lot of things. I needed to feel it, see it, hear it. And that's what I do—I see, I feel, I hear. I'm a physical empath . . . I didn't know that I had these abilities until, suddenly, I was experiencing them and then I had to understand them. I'm still learning to understand them . . ."

"Do you have a mantra that's like the 'control+alt+delete' for you that wipes out the old and brings in the new?" I asked. "A mantra that you feel vibrationally brings you to a level where you need to be?"

"I don't work with mantras, but the guides talk about claims of truth," he said. "They say that what they're working with is language that's encoded with vibrations—so if you work with a language, the language itself is going to work in your field in the energetic system in alignment with the claim that you make. They say when something is true, it's *always* true. So their claim, 'I know who I am, I know what I am, and I know how I serve,' is a claim of truth that they say calls you back into the present moment so that you're not choosing out of all the historical data and reactive impulse that we always have. If my first impulse is to kick the dog because I'm cranky, if I move back into present time, I can bypass that."

I know who I am. I know what I am. I know how I serve.

"The one that I'm working with from the new book is, 'I know who I am *in truth*, I know what I am *in truth*, I know how I serve *in truth*,' and the vibration of truth that they're working with now is really kind of kick-ass, I have to say! They're saying that truth is a field that you have to align to, and they say that in the vibration of truth a lie cannot be held."

In the vibration of truth, a lie cannot be held.

"And all of this fear-based stuff is essentially a lie," he said. "It's not who you truly are or who I truly am; it's what we've agreed to or what we've been taught. . . . At the end of *The Book of Mastery*, they say that they're leading their students up a mountain. It's a metaphor, and they say, 'So if there's stuff that you're still holding on to that's not moving, give it to us, and we will carry it for you, put it on the altar.' And I objected to it because I thought it sounded like enabling or magic or something, and they said, 'We operate as truth, and because we operate as truth, we cannot hold a lie. And the stuff that you are holding on to is lies. It's not who you truly are, so if you give it to us, at that level, they don't exist.' And that's now the teaching of the book of truth. . . . And frankly the things that I have dumped on the altar are working really well. The things I won't let go of are still causing me frustration."

"I think the human part of us would say that is a cop-out, 'Give it up to God or to the Universe,'" I said. "But by putting it on the altar, you are surrendering to the worry and you're saying, 'I don't see the answer clearly. I am sure it's coming or maybe it's behind a veil and I can't see it yet, so please pull back the curtain so I can embrace it?'"

"I don't know," Paul said. "I mean there are things that I'm really grappling with that I don't seem to want to let go of. Do I know they aren't the truth of who I am? Yes . . . I do get it sometimes, and when I really get it, I get it. And they talk about in *The Book of Mastery* that, 'The divine self is never persecuted' and that one I got. 'The divine self does not hold fear.' That one I really got. I'm not a proponent of magical thinking—I don't say, if you have bills to pay and you say, 'God's going to handle my bills, and I'm going to go off to the casino,' because I think you're going to screw yourself. The guides say we are responsible to all of our creations. The creations are the lives that we live. But how we attend to them, with whatever level of consciousness we tend to them, will impact the outcome."

As Paul was talking, he started to get *channeled information* from his guides that caused him to look to the side, use a deeper voice, and speak at lightning speed. It was fascinating to watch Paul flip back and forth between "Professor Paul" and "*Channel* Paul."

"When you're operating in a higher level of awareness or in an awareness of the divine self, how you create things first of all transforms because you're not creating in fear anymore. The guides say that *the action of fear is to claim more fear*. If you look at every challenge that you've made in your life and every choice you made because you were frightened, see what it got you. The guides are saying that *when you surrender . . . if you let go . . . it's in surrender . . .* if you still want it, you can have it . . . it's up to you."

"Does anything that happens to you while the channeling is happening frighten the human self, Paul?" I asked.

"No, not anymore," he said.

"You say in your book that even the murders are sparkles of light," I said. "I worked in the news business. Bad things happen. Talk about how hard it is to master the lesson that there are no bad things that happen—it just *is*."

"Thank God I haven't mastered it," he said. "I have had a lot in my life that is hard, and I don't think anyone gets out of this without pain—that's part of being here, and the guides that I work with are not teaching comfort and contentment. I mean my idea of comfort is a good movie on TV and a bag of cookies, and if I keep eating the cookies, I'm going to blow up to be even bigger than I am. So the whole idea that everything we encounter is an opportunity to learn and is an opportunity for growth reframes all of it. The idea that God is in everybody and everything, which is challenging, but the guides say again and again that you *cannot be the light and hold another in darkness.* You can't—it's the hypocrisy of religion! To say, 'God is only in the people who say and do as we do' is ridiculous."

I wanted to engrave this onto the foreheads of all my judgmental religious friends and relatives.

You cannot be the light and hold another in darkness.

"They say if there is a God, it's in all things," he said. "The awareness of this and the realization of this, they call that the Kingdom of Heaven: the awareness of the divine that is in all manifestation always, no matter what we think of it, and that's the hard part. It's easy to see the divine in your kid or the people who love you. It's a lot harder to see the divine in the people who hit your car or stole your money. Until we do, we are still sort of enforcing this paradigm of separation, which the guides are trying to move us out of. We all have the right to be—even the one who hit our car—we are all part of source. We were all born, so we all have a right to be. And most of us don't know this. They think we have the right to be 'IF' . . ."

You have the right to be IF you treat me with love and respect. Everyone else, please go somewhere else for Thanksgiving.

"I get a lot of flack from the religious crowd for the interviews that I do," I said. "I like to remind them that Jesus was a carpenter and not the CEO of Google. He went around from stump to stump teaching about love, tolerance, and healing. I wish they would act a little more Jesus-y. How did we get here? How did we get so disconnected from the source that was teaching us about love and healing?"

Paul sighed.

"I did a workshop at the Esalen Institute last May with a guy named Jeffrey Kripal, who is the head of the religious studies department at Rice University, and he's an expert on Gnosticism, and he wrote the introduction to *The Book of Mastery*," he said. "He's kind of an egghead on this subject, and he said that what my guides are teaching is actually second-century Christianity. This is old stuff. It's the essence of the teaching without the hierarchy institution attached. . . . The guides talked about it a bit in the new book . . . and they say the impulse to all religions was to lead us through a cycle towards enlightenment. But once churches had to start to survive and make money, they made all these rules and people got entrenched in these systems that had nothing to do with the original teaching."

"So how do we get back to that?" I asked.

Paul looked to the side, and the channeling began to flow.

"My guide just said, *By knowing who they are . . . in spite of their fear . . . because they're operating in fear. . . . When they believe that people are going to hell because of this or that . . . they are affirming fear . . . and God is not fear. . . . God is of source. . . . It is the one thing . . . that is never afraid. . . . It cannot hold the vibration. . . . Why do you wish to affirm that?? . . . There's nothing to it.* Their definition of Christ, and they unpack this in every book, they say the Christ is the aspect of the creator that can be realized in material form as who and what you all are. It's the God within. And they say Jesus realized this in fullness. And others have, they say, as well. That's a Christian teaching, so if people want to get upset about this stuff, they are welcome to it, but there's no fear in this. My guides don't tell people what to do; they do tell people what they are."

"For someone who was an atheist, to have these words like God and Christ coming through, how's that working for ya, Paul?" I asked.

"I've given up a little bit in how it seems," he said. "People who find the work that I do seem to be ready for the work that I do. But also I don't claim myself to be or consider myself to be a spiritual teacher or guru. I'm a guy who sits in a chair and takes this dictation."

"You say growth comes through discomfort, but so many people want to get back to the movies and cookies and get out of discomfort," I said.

"The guides say, *the allowance for it . . . many of you don't want it . . . so you run from it . . . and you claim it. The fear is what you are . . . it's not true . . . the allowance is key. . . . 'I allow myself to change . . . . I allow myself to know myself in a new way.' . . . This will support people . . . in creating the possibility . . . of change . . . with less discomfort. . . . The **allowance** is key.*"

"You say, 'the guides are teachers and the classroom is the world,' but for those who don't want to show up for school, this is where I have problems, Paul, with my judgment. What do the guides have to say about my judgment of those who aren't willing to show up?" I asked.

Paul looked off to the side and started to speak quickly.

"They're saying, *Trust them to be who they need to be for their own growth and don't prescribe. . . .* They're saying, *that's the challenge for you . . . you're presuming who they should be . . . and it's really up to them.*"

It's up to them to not SUCK.

"They're saying, when you know who somebody is in a higher way, 'I know who you are, I know what you are, I know how you serve.' You don't have to say it aloud. You are affirming that truth for them—claiming that for someone else in a vibratory accord. You're creating that alignment for them if they wish to assume it."

Paul then went on to explain how he was urged by his guides to get out of academia for years before he finally "came out" after twenty-five years of teaching at NYU.

"I was holding on like crazy," he said. "My benefits, my reputation. I didn't want people to know who I was and what I did. . . . It was a slow process for me to say, 'Okay this is it.' But I did when it was time, and I think I did it at exactly the right time for me. Had I done this ten years prior, the world might not have been ready for it, so I have to trust some of that."

I then asked about our belief systems and how they might impact our ability to manifest.

"My guides say we all have these frames which are belief systems, and we see the world through these frames and the purpose of the frame is to fulfill itself," he said. "If I say, 'All men are jerks,' and that's my frame, I'm going to keep calling men who are jerks into my frame. That's the job of the frame. You see we are always right. My guides say we are all in agreement to our landscape. Everything that you can see is something you're in agreement to. It couldn't be there at a level of co-residence without you. And that doesn't just include your personal life and circumstances. We've gotten a little too smug in the new age to think it's all about us or 'It's about me and my stuff and I'm creating my own reality.' We're in a shared reality and a shared construct, so if you can see it on the other side of the world, you're in agreement to it on some level of consciousness."

"Caroline Myss talks about how using a vision board for manifesting is very narcissistic," I said.

"I agree with her," he said. "You know, I've never met her, but right before I 'came out,' I was invited to hear her speak at Omega in New York, and I didn't know who she was. And I'm sitting there in the audience, and this little lady comes out and she starts yelling at everybody. And she says, 'You're all light workers—what are you doing sitting here in the dark? Get out there and do your work!' I was so shaken up by her that I actually had to leave. And I got home and said, 'Where am I going to find a group of forty people to read from at once?' So I opened up a chat room on AOL, and the only name I could find to read under was 'Second Sight.' I considered myself a clairaudient and clairsentient and channel, not someone who accessed visual stuff. And I worried people would ask, 'What do you see?' And the first person said, 'Second Sight, what do you see?' and all of the sudden I was seeing in Technicolor! I was telling people what they were wearing. I was having a ball. Within a year the guides were dictating through me. So I actually credit her, whom I've never met, for giving me a boot in the rump that got me out of my own fear of being seen for this."

The following week Paul was hosting a teleseminar online. While I would much rather see someone work in person, I wasn't able to attend his workshop in Chicago. To my surprise, I found this digital meeting to be very fulfilling.

"Professor Paul" sat on what seemed to be a couch in front of his computer and welcomed the group (who gathered together on Zoom). He said he didn't have any heads-up as to what the lecture would be, but that it would all come through the guides. Then, he became "Channel Paul" for about forty-five minutes, all while still seated. At the end of the message, "Professor Paul" would return to host the Q and A.

His channeled voice for the teleseminar was much more booming and deep than it was during our radio interview. He sounded a lot like Richard Burton performing Shakespeare at the Globe Theater in London. At times, his voice even quivered with vibrato.

The focus of the teaching was about seeing God in all things and lifting oneself up to the next level of creation. But to do this, we have to embrace the unknown no matter how it shows up.

"You stand on the pinpoint of all of your history," Channel Paul said. *"So you may dive from this place into the great unknown. Now why would you wish to do this, you may ask? Who wants that? 'I like my chair, I want my comfort, I want to know the money is in the bank, and the spouse is where I want him. I want to realize myself as long as I'm not challenged. I can't release the known. Just let me be a little more spiritual, I would be happy with that.' Those days are over, we say. If you want your peace, and you seek to find it in yesterday's news, you will be looking a very long time. Now there is nothing wrong with being grateful for what you have, the husband and the kids and the job you go to, and the resources you have, but when you step into the unknown, you're actually claiming the new. We are not telling you to leave the lives you've known as much as to claim the unknown—to welcome it as where you go next—even at the cost of those things you've used to prescribe as your identity.*

"As the manifestation of God in man is agreed to by more and more of you, the energetic alignment you hold will be matched in circumstance in the physical reality that is perceived

by you. . . . To those of you who are new, when you believe your-
self as separate, distinct, physical energy, physical manifestation
of source but source is not AS you, then source is not in anything
you see. If everything is God, high and low and in between, in
form, this must require that the form YOU hold is divine as
well. And this is an energetic agreement to be AS truth—under-
line the word AS. In form. Truth in form. And the vibration
YOU hold at that level can be in agreement to the truth that's
in form in everything you see BEFORE you.

"When you know what you are, you know what all things
are as well. . . . The same VIBRATION that HOLDS every
molecule together that you know as your body, HOLDS every-
thing else together, you cannot be separate from its being. You
are not separate from your source. And the knowing of THIS is
what alchemizes you, aligns you in physical form to the level of
manifestation that we call alchemy and manifestation in form.
On this night we wish you and ALL OF YOU the gift of real-
ization. That your hands may be used, your heart may be sung,
your eyes may see, the divine IN ALL.

"The song we sing for you tonight is the song of change. The
song we wish for you tonight is the song of great knowing and in
knowing you may see, and when you see, you may claim it and
be as you truly are. I sing the song of yes. Yes I am. Yes I be. Yes
I know. To all I witness in this new life. I know who I am in
truth, I know what I am in truth, I know how I serve in truth.
I am here. I am here. I am here. We are with you now, each of
you yes, those of you who are feeling your field shiver are feeling
the agreement form—the field that you hold releasing expecta-
tions, so the unknown and the glory of the unknown may be

*known as and through you. You cannot know God in its full-
ness. It is too vast. It is the unknown in perfection. But you may
know it as you witness it in the world before you. In the skin on
your hand, the eyes of your friend, your child, in your neighbor,
in the ones before you, the divine is present in all. In all.*

*"There are only two levels of intent: Love or fear. Something
that is made in love will stand firmly throughout all change.
Something that was made in fear must be re-created or re-known
in truth to stand the change that will come."*

After the channel, "Professor Paul" took a handful of
questions. The last one came from a woman named Connie.

"So is the easy answer that we are supposed to let go and
say 'yes' and let the divine self run?" she asked.

"Yes! But not the way you think," Channel Paul said. *"Not
at the cost of not paying your bills and not showing up at the
office unless the divine self leads you another way. It's not a
teaching of being lazy—it's a teaching of agreeing to the truth.
And at that level, remarkable things happen. You've received a
teaching tonight into the unknown. Say 'thank you' to it. That
it may bring you what you NEED outside of what you would
prescribe it to do, because the one who prescribes is the small self.
It calls what she thinks she needs, based on what she was told to
have. And what we would have in store would be remarkably
better. Thank you each for your presence. We will say goodnight.
He may say goodnight if he wishes. We will see you next week."*

A week later, I arranged a time to have my reading with
Paul. While he was fine doing it over the phone, I wanted

to see his face in case he took on any of the characteristics of the people I asked about during our conversation, so we set up a time to Skype.

"So as you work, will you be seeing, hearing, or feeling your information?" I asked, looking at an image of "Professor Paul" on my computer screen.

"I hear, and when I hear, I whisper the words as they come and repeat them so you're going to hear things twice," Paul said. "Sometimes I'm hearing you or an aspect of you. Other times I hear the people you are asking me about. And other times I'm hearing my guides, and I'm just taking dictation or channeling. If I'm not hearing clearly, I'll tell you that, too."

"Deal," I said.

"So if you could tell me your full name, and then we can get started," he said.

"Jenniffer Colleen Weigel," I said.

Paul took a few deep breaths, and then began.

"You're like this [he puts up his fists], so you're so ready to fight right now and you're looking in front of you like, 'What's it gonna be?' Your dukes are up not really to hit anybody but as a way to sort of manage. Like 'I have to be strong and handle this.' It's in relationship to 'What am I doing? What can I have? What can I make happen?' And also, 'What's their problem?' Do you understand this?"

"Yes," I said, thinking that he had just nailed how I feel every moment of every day in my world as a freelance writer and divorced, single mom.

"So let's see how you can move through this," he said. "Okay, you're telling me, 'The first thing I have to do is get out of my own way, and I forget how to get out of my own way.'"

Damn!

"It's like I'm looking at your path and there's a great big yellow tractor sitting right in the middle of it, and you just want to yell at the tractor but that's not how it moves," he said. "How does it move? The guides say, '*Thank you, tractor, for moving.*' Like you don't battle it, you say, '*Thank you for moving. I'm ready to move.*' It gets to move. *That's allowance.* But you have this feeling that you have to rail against the world in order for change to happen. This is exhausting you."

I'll say.

"My sense is that you have been experiencing change in every area of your life," he said.

I'd moved, switched jobs, and had a relationship come to an end in the last few months, so this was spot-on.

"The guides are saying '*productively*' and that's what you can't see," he said. "Like 'This is really productive.' But I don't know that you will see it until you're on the other side of that damn tractor."

Can you get one of those guides to stop yapping so they can move the stupid tractor?!

"I'm going to ask what the tractor means," he said. "Some of this frankly is about your industry, your work, everything you've had to do for yourself, and I feel like it's just there. It's in the way. Why? Because everybody told you what the fuck to do and you listened. That's part of the problem."

Are his guides the ones swearing or is that my higher self?

"You listened to other people, so this is the outcome," he said. "What I tune in to first is usually the landscape that you're currently in."

Not a big fan of this landscape, Paul!

"What would you like to know?" he asked.

"Well, how can I make progress if the tractor is in my way?" I asked.

"Right now I feel as you that I'm so kind of overwhelmed that all I want to do is yell at it and that's not what moves the energy," he said. "Allowance. Forgiveness. And stepping out of the way. Let the tractor move out of the way and then you can walk."

I felt like I was back in Echo's reading, duct taped to the high chair wearing sunglasses.

"You're stepping out of the way to *allow* for this to happen versus *making* it happen," he said. "What else would you like to know?"

I got out my list of folks and asked Paul a few specifics. I was totally amazed at how he turned into these people, both physically and vocally. His imitation of my mother's pitch and inflection was so accurate I thought she had entered my living room.

You can't Google my mom's tone of voice and tempo.

When I asked about my son, Paul's face seemed to change shape and his eyes also went from hazel to very light blue. When he stopped talking about my son, his eyes went back to hazel. It was freaky, to say the least.

"I feel when I am your son, it's like, 'Nobody's telling me the truth. They want things to look better and they're not better,'" he said. "This kid wants you to tell him the truth."

Both my ex and I kept Britt in the dark when things got stressful with our divorce. We were learning now that this actually wasn't the best move.

"My sense is that what he imagines is often worse than the reality," he said. "So your withholding puts him in the position to make things up, and what he makes up is based on the frame of reference of a ten-year-old, which is more black and white than reality. Love your son and let him form his own thoughts. Affirm everything that's productive for him. Affirm it and give him strength through affirmation. He's confused now, but it will play itself out."

Okay, so that's ALLOW for the tractor, and AFFIRM for my son. Got it.

"Do you see a relationship coming up for me?" I asked.

"Yes, I hear quickly if you're open to it," he said. "You're grabbing someone at a party and saying, 'Let's have some fun. Why not? It's been a hell of a year. We deserve it.' I think this is someone in your industry. A work colleague."

Note to self: Go to more media parties.

"It's good and easy, and that's what you need," he said. "You really don't need the pressure of a relationship, but you do want the comfort of the availability of something right now. You're thinking, 'I've got enough change, if somebody shows up that I can enjoy, I want to enjoy it. That's enough right now. If there's more there, we'll sort that out as it happens.'"

"I seem to have a challenge where I attract people who keep secrets," I said. "I wonder if there's a time when the guides can see if I framed that up in my belief system?"

"Yeah," he said, without hesitation. "I go to your childhood. I heard six years old with this one."

When my parents were getting divorced, they often used me as a spy. It was very dysfunctional, but it definitely sparked my desire to be a reporter and gather facts at a very young age.

"You are saying to me, 'I actually don't choose people who have secrets. They create them in order to be in response to me,'" he said. "In a certain way you're expecting it, so they deliver. The Universe doesn't understand 'no,' so if you say 'I'm never going to date an alcoholic,' guess who's going to date one?"

"So for all those years when I would think, 'I never want to be with someone who keeps secrets,' I created the space for people to come in and not be trustworthy because that was what I was putting out there?!" I asked.

"Yes," he said.

UGH!

"Let me see if there's anything I can do around this," he said, getting quiet for a few moments. "Thank everybody for being who they are, no matter what they represent. What this actually does is dismantle the need for the lie—the need to be betrayed. There's a little bit of a need there because it provokes a wound. This is about betrayal, which is more than a secret. You're explaining it to me. If you don't have the need for a certain dynamic, then you have no expectations on them or how they're supposed to be and that includes the negative. Expect them to be who they are, and then you are operating in a much clearer landscape."

So I can't even have standards?

"Let me ask if there's anything else they would like to tell you," he said. "*The only thing we would like to say to this young lady is she has to stop telling herself that she can't have what she wants. It's actually a problem now.* You're looking at your feet saying, 'What am I gonna get?' But it's becoming a mantra of 'What am I not receiving yet?' and that's a bit of a challenge. What's the remedy for this? *'Thank you, thank you, thank you. I receive, I receive, I receive. I'm allowed, I'm allowed, I'm allowed.'* I want to say to myself, 'Easier said than done.'"

Yes!

"The guides say that I, Paul, do the same thing, but I enjoy it," Paul said. "I enjoy not getting what I want, they say. That's not your problem. "

An enlightened channel such as Paul Selig prevents himself from getting what he wants?

I was beginning to realize that not even a powerful intuitive is immune to self-sabotage because they, too, are still human.

"So back to you," Paul said. "Some of this is patience and having enough faith to realize that everything is moving even when it feels like it isn't. And take a deep breath. About all of it—the divorce, the job changes, the living situation. When your focus is off what happened, there's a kind of peace that's available to you that I don't know that you've

had for some time. It's a quiet peace. Not lonely, just easy.
Peaceful. That's the right, next place for you."

I receive. I allow. Thank you.

7

Dr. Judith Orloff

GROWING UP WITH INTUITIVE ABILITIES ISN'T easy when your parents work in the medical field.

"I come from a family of twenty-five physicians," said Judith Orloff, MD. "As a child, I had extreme intuition; I would have premonitions. I would be able to sense when someone was going to die or when there was a divorce happening with my parents' friends. I could predict earthquakes—all kinds of scary things. So my parents got very alarmed. They were both physicians. They forbade me from talking about my intuition at home. I grew up believing there was something wrong with me."

Judith spent most of her teenage years trying to "escape" her intuition with drugs and alcohol.

"I would try to numb myself out, which of course doesn't work," she said. "I finally was sent to a psychiatrist who helped me see that I had to integrate my intuitions and all facets of myself to become whole. I couldn't run away from myself anymore, even when I went into medical school. I'd been 'in the closet' with my intuition, and then to come out, it's a wonderful thing to teach other people who are empathic."

Judith's mother continued to struggle with her daughter's gifts her entire life. As she was close to dying, her mother finally admitted that Judith came from a long lineage of intuitive female healers. After decades of defending her gifts to her family (and especially to her mother), Judith was finally validated.

Now the author of five best-selling books, including *Positive Energy*, *Emotional Freedom*, and *The Power of Surrender*, Judith is a board-certified psychiatrist and assistant professor of psychiatry at UCLA. She does workshops throughout the year teaching people to develop their intuition and healing abilities, and lives in the Los Angeles area.

I'd interviewed Judith several times, both in person and over the phone, since I began working as a journalist in the 1990s. Her first book, *Positive Energy* (which has been translated into twenty-three languages), was one of those life-changing reads that I carried with me for weeks. Her take on "energy vampires," people who "suck the life out of you," really hit home. She also discussed how to shift energy from negative to positive in very simple ways, from picturing white light around your body to letting people cut in front of you in line. Even dropping a five-dollar bill on the floor of the bathroom for others to find can make a difference. To this day, I always think of Judith when I leave money on the floor in public places.

In the spring of 2016, Judith was my guest for my podcast "I'm Spiritual, Dammit!" She had just released her *Power of Surrender* cards, which is a fifty-two-card deck of inspirational messages based on her writings. I've been a fan of Doreen Virtue's Angel Cards for years and often pulled one here and there to see what came up. Judith's deck had deep messages that all began with "Surrender." So whether it's "Surrender Procrastination" or "Surrender the Drama," you think of a topic where you need guidance and then pull a card.

"This is a great way to get children to embrace their intuition because it's fun," Judith said during our interview. She was on the phone in Los Angeles, while I was in the studio back in Chicago.

"What would you say to parents of intuitive children to help them better understand what's going on for their child?" I asked.

"Ask your children how they feel about things and if they have a gut feeling about certain things," she said. "Keep it very light and very matter-of-fact. Also try to help them remember their dreams and ask them, 'What did you dream last night?' Whenever I have people stay at the house, I always have dream circles in the mornings. Dreams offer you intuitive solutions you would never think of while awake. That's why it's so important to be open to different aspects of intuition—the dream life, the gut feeling, sensing energy, the 'aha' moments. Paul McCartney talks about the 'aha' moments when he had a dream about his songs and how he uses his dreams and intuition to write. And Steve Jobs said intuition is the primary skill that led him to success in business. We can't ignore it."

"Are we jumping into meds too quickly these days with our sensitive children?" I asked.

"Great question," she said. "People come to me with this when they have intuitive children, and my preference is always to *not* go the medication route. Sometimes you need to—sometimes a person's serotonin levels are so low you have to give a pharmacological intervention to raise it. But that isn't always the case, and I think so many psychiatrists, especially with sensitive people, jump in so quickly to medicate that it's just wrong. There are other ways to deal with high sensitivity other than medicating. Like meditating. And you have to teach children to calm down. They don't know how to do that. They have a lot of frenetic energy. So through breathing, through centering, through being in nature, being with animals. Learning to tune in to people who make you feel good when they are around rather than being around energy vampires where you're absorbing all sorts of toxic energy from people."

"Do you think a lot of what kids are facing today is anxiety?" I asked.

"Yes, I'm an empath, and what that means is that I sense people's stress and anxiety, and I tend to absorb it in my body because I don't have the usual defenses that people have," she said. "So you must learn strategies such as meditation and exercising and tuning in—really centering yourself—so the anxiety doesn't throw you off."

"What are the best ways to protect yourself from energy vampires?" I asked.

"You have to practice visualizing a shield around you," she said. "It could be red light or white light—whatever you want. But picture it about six inches away from your body, and this helps keep other people's residue or anger, frustration, malice, depression, whatever is floating around the air energetically, away from you. And then get in water as soon as possible. Get in a bath or a shower, because water is purifying.

"Also just know that whatever you absorb from other people—for instance if you absorb anger from other people around you and you feel it's a knife going into your gut—then most likely you haven't dealt with all of your own anger issues. You might be suppressing it. When you work through a lot of your psychological issues, you can sense the energy—the anger energy—and it can be depleting, but it's not like a knife in your gut. It doesn't go that deep if you've worked on yourself, and therefore it doesn't drain you."

"You talk about using 'soft power' to deal with the anger addict and not taking in or absorbing someone else's rage or anger, but standing in the light and saying, 'I can see how you might feel that way,' but you're not taking it in," I said. "It's valuable when I can remember to do it!"

"It's SO valuable, but that's not the only strategy with dealing with the anger addict," she said. "I have a no yelling rule in my house. I'm sensitive. I can't take it. If people want to yell, they can go elsewhere. I can express anger but not yelling. Yelling to me is dumping. You have to set limits in your own house. Some people feel better after they yell. Being an empath, you have to be able to say 'no' and set boundaries and do your best to do this with them in a kind but loving way. Be firm but loving."

"I asked author and medium James Van Praagh, 'If there was one thing you wished people could remember more often, what would that be?' and he said he wished we could remember how our energy field is affected by other people's sludge," I said. "Unconsciously we pick it up, even if we're just walking through a hotel lobby. If we are unconscious, he said, our energy field looks like the lint roller that you roll on somebody's carpet who has five cats. And the way to get rid of it is to consciously take what he calls a 'light shower' or what you suggest, an actual shower. Or if you're driving, picture yourself taking a light shower and having all that bad energy and sludge go down the drain and back to the light for healing and get it off of you. Would you agree?"

"Yes, I think that's great, but I also think people need to step up and set boundaries," she said. "Learn how to do it with your eyes, with your voice, and be very clear with your energy. If you want to develop your intuition, you have to be able to set boundaries with people, because otherwise they're going to walk all over your energy field. You're going to feel like a doormat emotionally and energetically. As a psychiatrist, I work with my patients on how to not let that happen and be strong and intuitive. And just say 'no' to people. But people will write constantly and ask, 'What do I do if my mother is living with me or my husband is depressed and I can't get away?' Then you do the best you can with the boundary setting and take alone time for yourself and replenish yourself and work to compromise with these people."

"What if you're dealing with a narcissist?" I asked.

"Narcissists are an exception," she said. "I write a lot about narcissists in all my books because I feel so strongly that they are toxic influences on any intuitive person. Narcissists have empathy-deficient disorder. They don't have empathy. It's so hard for sensitive people to get this. I'm talking the full-blown narcissists. They basically don't care what you're feeling, and that's so hard for loving people to get because narcissists are so charming. They know how to say everything to reel you in and touch your buttons and seemingly love you. They're so intelligent, so much fun, until there's a conflict or until you do something that doesn't go along with their plan. Then they become cold, withholding, and punishing. Empaths and sensitive and intuitive people believe that they can change the narcissist with their love. That's the hook. The intuitive feels that they are going to be taken care of by the narcissist, and the narcissist loves the sensitivity of the intuitive because they are such a caretaker and have a big heart. I've had many a patient who has tried that, and I wish everyone would just trust me—you can't do it! I've had people get angry at me and say, 'Don't you believe in the power of love?' Sure I do, intensely and passionately, but not with these people because they're not able to dialogue with you. They are not able to present their authentic selves. Part of healing is facilitated by the people you have around you. If you have really beautiful loving supportive people around you, it will help you grow, and it will help you on your path. If you have a lot of narcissists or energy vampires, it's a different challenge. But keep moving on and find the empath and intuitive tribe. We need to have our people around us."

A few weeks later, I was heading to Los Angeles for some meetings and set up a time to get together with Judith.

Flying into LAX was uneventful, but getting my rental car was an entirely different drama. The shuttle took thirty minutes to show up, and when it arrived, it was overbooked. Our cars were located miles from the airport, and when we were finally dropped off at the rental car location, the staff was about as energetic as a group of hibernating bears.

This is what you get for booking things last minute, Jen.

As I was waiting in line for what seemed to be three years, I pulled out Judith's Surrender Cards.

Show me what I need to know right now, Universe.

I shuffled the cards around in my hands and pulled one out. It was the "Surrender to Divine Timing" card, with a message that read: "Sometimes divine timing may differ from your ego's timing. If a goal isn't manifesting 'fast enough' according to your ego, be patient and trust the universal flow."

Be patient, Jen.

Eventually, I got my car, which had stains on the seats, dings on the doors, and barely reached forty-five miles an hour when I floored the gas pedal. I quickly put the address of my hotel in the GPS and got into traffic.

Chateau Marmont, here I come.

I have a friend Phil who has worked at the famous Chateau Marmont hotel for over twenty years. He started off as a guy at the front desk and worked his way up to managing director. Whenever I head to L.A. for meetings, if there's room at the Chateau, I'm there. The location is perfect and the people-watching is priceless.

When I arrived, I pulled in to the driveway, and found myself stopped behind a guy in a Maserati.

One of these things is not like the other . . .

The valet walked over to my car and gave it the once over.

"Are you picking someone up?" he asked.

"I'm actually checking in," I said to his surprise.

"Oh, then you can leave the keys with me," he said looking less than enthused.

"I bet this is the first KIA to enter the Chateau garage, huh?" I said.

"Oh, I bet there has been one before," he said with a laugh.

I got out of the car and noticed a man standing by the valet stand smoking a cigarette. He kind of looked like a disheveled version of Sean Penn. As I grabbed my luggage, I walked past him and got a closer look.

"Nice coat," he said, referring to my red raincoat.

"Thanks," I said.

Oh, shit! That actually IS Sean Penn!

I arrived at the front desk, and a beautiful model with a British accent (that may or may not have been fake) checked me in.

"We actually *just* got word that we are able to upgrade you to a bigger room," she said.

If I'd arrived even ten minutes earlier, I wouldn't have gotten the upgrade.

Surrender to Divine Timing.

The room they gave me wasn't just bigger; it was an actual apartment complete with a kitchen and living room.

Hot damn!

I interviewed author Pam Grout, who had penned several best-selling books, including one of my favorites, E^2, where she talks about our ability to manifest our desires. In order to start making room for things you want, you have to act "as if" you deserve it. Pam said she bought a dress that was *a little* out of her price range to "make a statement to the Universe" that she was worth that and many more expensive dresses.

Even the smallest room at the Chateau Marmont was *a little* out of my price range, and now I found myself with the kind of accommodations they only give famous people.

Act as if, Jen.

That night I went to dinner with several friends from high school I hadn't seen in years.

"So who are you interviewing tomorrow?" my friend Elizabeth asked. Liz and I had been very close when we were teenagers, but the distance of living in different parts of the country prevented us from being in better touch.

"Dr. Judith Orloff," I said. "She's a psychiatrist who believes in the power of intuition and believes that if we listen to our body, we can learn everything from why we are sick to which people we can trust."

"I actually totally believe that," Liz said.

"Really?" I said, getting excited I had a kindred spirit.

"I went for my physical last fall and my doctor told me everything was totally fine, but I just had this *feeling* that something wasn't right," she said. "I said to my doctor, 'Can you just check my thyroid? I really think there might be something going on.' I don't know why, but I was so sure something was up with my thyroid. So she did some tests and called me in. It turns out I actually had thyroid cancer."

"What?!" I said, not knowing she had fought any disease at all, let alone thyroid cancer.

"Yes, I know," she said. "I knew something wasn't right. They removed my thyroid, and I'm on medication and everything looks good now. But if I hadn't listened to my body, who knows what would have happened."

"Even when your tests come out clean, there can be something wrong," I said.

"Exactly," she said.

Thank God she listened to her body!

The next day, it was time to see Judith.

As I waited for my KIA at the valet, I noticed a beautiful woman standing next to me. She had ivory skin and red lips. I'm not a lesbian, but this woman was so pretty, I would have made out with her in a hot minute.

That kind of looks like Kate Beckinsale.

A Mercedes SUV came up the driveway and parked. I watched as that gorgeous thing gracefully entered the vehicle.

That IS Kate Beckinsale!

Just then, my chariot arrived.

Beep beep!

"Here you are," the valet said, struggling to get out of my tiny rental.

"Thanks," I said, trying not to blush in embarrassment.

You're just as worthy as Kate Beckinsale, Jen. Act as if.

When I got closer to the ocean, I had some trouble figuring out the directions to Judith's home. She lived in an area where some streets don't allow cars. The more I worried, the farther I seemed to get from my destination. I then thought about Judith's theory of surrendering, and how *wanting* something so much can block the energy from making it happen. I looked up at the sky and started yapping.

Hey, Universe, I totally surrender to finding Judith's house.

I sat at the light tapping my toes to Bruno Mars when suddenly a text came through. It was Judith giving me

step-by-step directions of how to find her from the intersec-
tion where I was currently sitting in traffic.

That was fast!

I arrived at Judith's home, parked in her driveway, and
she greeted me at the back gate.

"Hello!" she said, giving me a hug.

Judith has bright blue eyes and brown shoulder-length
hair with blue streaks in the back. She wore leggings, and
a sheer, linen long-sleeved shirt covering her tank top. As
I entered her home, I was immediately soothed by all the
beautiful colors. There were bright blues and reds and pur-
ples in everything from the tiles to the throw pillows.

"Let's sit in here," she said, guiding me to her sun-filled
living room.

"Your house is gorgeous," I said, looking at her floor-to-
ceiling windows and feeling the peace and comfort of her
space.

"Thank you!" she said. "I love it by the water."

Judith's voice was soft and nurturing. If I lived in Los
Angeles (and was able to get on her waiting list), I would do
whatever it took to have her as my therapist.

"Your house has such a sense of calm," I said. "What's
your daily ritual or daily mantra to keep you connected to
spirit or source every day?"

"I listen to the Great Bell Chant from Thich Nhat
Hanh," she said. "That does it for me to get me centered. I
also practice the Three-Minute Heart Meditation. I practice
that every day. I also wake up with a gratitude affirmation
every day."

"What about before bed?" I asked.

"Water," she said. "My sacred ritual of a bath and having quiet time before sleep is so important to me."

"From your journey and looking at your body of work, do you think differently about anything that you've written in the past, or is everything still in alignment with your current belief systems?" I asked.

"I think my beliefs have deepened," she said. "Especially with fear in terms of the power of fear to separate one from spirit and how that fear accumulates over a period of time. And in terms of intuition and energy, that fear can stack up with so many people that it can have enormously detrimental effects on people. So I think it's important to know and understand that so you can keep your connection to spirit current always. That is the most important thing."

Keep your connection to spirit current always.

"I seem to get torn between surrendering and then feeling like I'm not doing enough," I said. "If I really want something to happen, I feel like you have to do something about it."

"You do need to put things in motion," Judith said. "But you also need to surrender the outcome if you aren't seeing progress. If you want something too much, you can actually stop it from coming to you and block the energy."

Note to self: Stop wanting things too much!

"Do you think everybody has a persistent soul challenge that they are brought in to heal and work on?" I asked.

"Sure," she said.

"Do you know what some of yours are?" I asked.

"Well, I've been in a relationship about three years now, and I think the biggest challenge is just being my natural empathic self with somebody and learning how to balance being with somebody and *not* being with somebody, which is extremely difficult," she said. "It's very hard to find the balance. But one thing I've learned is the importance of speaking up for my intuition or my empathic needs and my tendency for sensory overload. If I'm in sensory overload, I'm no good to anybody. It's been a challenge because a human being brings with them certain energies versus being alone. When I'm alone, I can totally control my environment in terms of input. I have a deep yearning to be in connection to a partner, yet at the same time, I have a lot of difficulty in regulating the input."

"When you get your intuitive information on people, is it clairaudient or clairvoyant?" I asked.

"It's more of an inner knowing," she said. "The way I tune in is I close my eyes and then I go inward to connect to my heart. And as a result of that, my awareness expands and I'm able to tune in to something greater than my ego. That's all I do. So with my patients, I tune in and I get information, and then I weave it into the therapy session."

"You are the ultimate combo platter because you weave science in with your intuition," I said. "For those who are skeptical of the fact that our emotions can affect our health, what would you say to those people? If someone tells you, 'I just don't get it,' how would you try to get them to get it?"

"I wouldn't," she said.

Excuse me?

"I would just work within their belief systems and see how they can be happier within their own framework," she said. "I've never tried to convince people of anything. Like this one teenager didn't want to come in and see me, and her mother dragged her in. At the end of the session she really connected with me and asked if she could come back, and I said, 'Only if you want to. If she's dragging you here, then I don't want you here.' If people don't want to work on something, then God bless them and go somewhere else. If they don't want to look under the hood, you can't make them. It's not my job. And maybe it's best for them not to look under the hood right now."

"So even when you encounter other physicians who aren't quite on board with the power of intuition, you don't try to convince them?" I asked.

"It's not my job to convince them," she said. "It's just my job to offer what has worked for me, and maybe it will work for them and, if not, then so be it."

Surrender, surrender, surrender.

"What are your thoughts on manifesting?" I asked. "Some people believe that suffering could be part of your divine path, and other teachers don't think suffering needs to happen at all."

"I think you can limit the amount of suffering you have with your attitude and how you perceive things," she said. "You can make it worse for yourself. People suffer differently. Some people suffer in very difficult ways, and other people suffer more lightly. It depends on what your style is."

"Is suffering a choice?" I asked.

"How much you suffer is a choice," she said. "You can make it worse or make it better. And I don't think it's right to focus on suffering all the time, but I also don't think it's right to think there isn't suffering. Hopefully you want to create more joy and gratitude, even when you're suffering."

"Do you still put money on the floor?" I asked.

"Yeah, I do, and I throw all the pennies into the street, too," she said. "I'm a big believer in the ability to shift energy in chaotic, crowded places, just by doing a deed of kindness for somebody, which can shift the energy. In L.A., there is so much traffic, so just letting someone into the lane in front of you, they can't believe it because nobody lets anybody in."

"I notice that sometimes I have a reaction that is really huge to something very small," I said. "For example, if someone doesn't include me in social plans, because of my abandonment issues, I can go to 'Defcon 5.'"

"If you are super reactive to something, that means something inside you isn't healed," she said. "But that is part of knowing that everyone has trigger points, and so if you work on them, someone can push those buttons but it won't cut so deep. But listen to your body, because if you try to micromanage too much with your mind, you cut out the channeling and the healing energy. It's about flowing and trusting and always listening to the body about getting 'yeses' and 'nos' about things—what feels right, what doesn't, and trusting that implicitly."

As I got back to my hotel, I was overwhelmed by a scene that looked like it came right out of TMZ, complete with a red carpet, paparazzi, and skinny people standing around with clipboards.

I drove as close as I could to the hotel entrance, and some huge security guard leaned into my car window.

"Sorry, this is a private party," he said, oozing with attitude.

"I'm actually staying here," I said.

Act as if, Jen.

"Oh, okay then," he said, stepping to the side. "Pull up to the valet."

I pulled in, and saw my valet buddy from check-in.

"I know you missed me," I said, happy to see a familiar face.

"Welcome back," he said, taking my KIA keys into custody.

As I walked into the lobby, there *was* a full-blown party taking over the first floor. Two gorgeous women who looked like they were about fourteen stood at the top of the stairs with a stapled list in their hands.

"Can I have your name, please?" one of them asked.

"I'm staying here," I said, showing them my room key as validation.

"Oh, welcome back," she said, feigning a smile.

"What's going on tonight?" I asked.

"It's a premiere party for the movie *Love and Friendship*," she said.

"Isn't that starring Kate Beckinsale?" I asked, looking around the crowd for my new favorite movie star.

"Yes," she said. "Help yourself to a cocktail."

"Thank you," I said, making my way into the party.

Act as if, Jen.

As I headed to the bar, a woman walked past me and smiled.

"I love your jacket," she said referring to my favorite red raincoat.

She kind of looks like Chloë Sevigny.

"Thank you," I said.

That IS Chloë Sevigny.

I took my drink upstairs to enjoy the view of Sunset Boulevard and opened my emails.

Once again, there was a note from a skeptic begging me to stop interviewing so many "crazy" mediums and psychics to protect my reputation as a journalist.

Why can't these people leave me alone?

I thought about the words of Judith and how she said it wasn't her job to convince other physicians to use their intuition.

"It's just my job to offer what has worked for me, and maybe it will work for them and, if not, then so be it."

I grabbed my Surrender card deck out of my purse and shuffled them around.

Show me the card I need, Universe.

I pulled out a card and looked.

Surrender Frustration: *Frustration doesn't open any doors. The key to resolving a dilemma or dissolving a* *block is to take a breath, center yourself, and regroup so you may approach the situation more calmly.*

I took my last sip of wine, and turned off my computer. *I surrender the frustration.*

The following morning, I opened my door to get my newspaper. (Yes, I still read those.) While the *New York Times* was nowhere to be found, I did find a fruit basket and two very large bottles of European water—one sparkling and one still. Inside the basket was an envelope that read: "Ms. Beckinsale."

OMG!

While Kate Beckinsale's care package was obviously delivered to my room by mistake, Pam Grout would've been proud of my manifesting skills.

Way to act "as if," Jen!

I took a picture and texted it to my little sister.

"Room service accidentally gave me Kate Beckinsale's goody basket!" I wrote.

"That is SO your life!" she wrote back, followed by a variety of smiley faced emojis. "Did you keep the water at least?"

"Absolutely," I responded.

8

Caroline Myss

CAROLINE MYSS CAME INTO MY LIFE in 2001, at a time when I was in career crisis. My father had just died of a brain tumor, and I had somehow been tipped off to her first book, *Anatomy of the Spirit*. In this work, she chronicled her journey of embracing her ability to diagnose illness by using her intuition rather than the usual medical tests or tools.

Caroline wanted to be a journalist and a fiction writer, so this medical intuitive stuff was pretty inconvenient.

"Nobody did this kind of work, so I didn't really know *what* to call it," she said.

Eventually, Caroline "came out" in 1983, and soon started working with Dr. Norm Shealy, a Harvard-trained brain surgeon who partnered with her to diagnose patients. *Anatomy of the Spirit* flew off the shelves, and her second book *Sacred Contracts* soon followed, which also became a *New York Times* best seller.

I was working at CBS in Chicago as a reporter and anchor when *Sacred Contracts* was released. Unfortunately for me, I knew that my job was the furthest thing from my sacred contract, focusing on the problems of the world, rather than finding solutions.

Everything sucks, now back to you in the studio.

When I got word that Caroline was coming to a local bookstore in Chicago, I begged my producer to let me do an interview. Caroline's status as a best-selling author was the only reason my producer agreed.

A winter storm blanketed the city with several inches of snow on the day of my interview, so I was the only television reporter who showed up. Of course, I had to promise my producer we would still get to our live shot a couple of hours later or the deal was off.

It's snowing outside, back to you in the studio.

When I got to the bookstore, Caroline greeted me with a warm smile.

"Very nice to meet you," she said.

She was petite, had a firm handshake, and wore a cashmere sweater with pearls. She looked me straight in the eyes as she spoke.

"So when I read this book, it was like a lightbulb went off for me," I said. "Follow your instincts, because it's probably your destiny calling!"

"A lot of people resonate with the concept," Caroline said. "Now whether or not they follow through with it is another story."

"Why do you think it's so hard for people to follow through with their sacred contracts?" I asked.

"What I've discovered, Jenniffer, is that most people are terrified to take a look at all they can be," she said. "And the reason is because they'd have to act on it. People are afraid of the responsibility that comes with knowing yourself more deeply. People will even sabotage their own success because they're afraid. You're afraid of the hard work."

"Maybe they aren't afraid of success, but they're afraid of not being able to make a living," I said. "I know television news isn't my dream job, but it's paying the mortgage right now and I just can't throw that away."

'Yes, you can pay the bills doing what you are doing now," she said. "But if you don't follow through with your contracts, you will pay for it physically and emotionally. . . . If you move in the direction of following your purpose, the rest will fall into place. . . . As soon as you move into your contracts, people who are supposed to come into your life will show up. I truly believe that our lives are choreographed and flow from a combination of choice and destiny."

A couple of months after that conversation, I wound up leaving television news because I felt life was too short to hate your job. While my interview with Caroline wasn't the reason for my departure, her words certainly helped give me the strength to stick to my guns.

Thankfully, I haven't had to say, "It's cold outside, now back to you in the studio," in years.

As my journalism career took me from television news, to talk radio, and finally to my years of working as a newspaper columnist, Caroline and I always stayed in touch. I'd interview her about her latest books, and she would give me advice on everything from my divorce to speaking engagements. We got into the habit of having dinner every couple of months to catch up.

One hot day in June 2015, Caroline was planning to come meet me at work. Since she herself had been a journalist and editor, she'd always wanted to tour the inside of the *Chicago Tribune*, which was rich with history and located in the heart of downtown Chicago on Michigan Avenue.

"Come down at around four, and after the tour, we can grab some dinner," I wrote in an email.

"Deal," she replied.

I got clearance to bring a guest into the building and made reservations at my favorite Italian restaurant around the corner. Everything was perfectly lined up. There was just *one* small wrinkle to our grand plan.

I was fired before lunch.

Shit!

Thinking I had actually been called in for a raise and a promotion, I walked out of the building in complete shock and called Caroline.

"I think we should do this another day," she said.

"No," I said, realizing that my ability to have *anyone* tour the premises would be over in a couple weeks. "We sure as hell can't do it after I'm gone. Let's do this today."

"You go get some air, and call me in a couple of hours," she said. "It's going to be okay, kiddo. I mean it."

Caroline always calls me *kiddo*.

I walked across the street and started mumbling to myself.

I can't believe this is happening.

I made my way to a pathway along the Chicago River and stared out at the water. I'd looked at this view a thousand times, and for some reason, I was seeing it for the first time.

What gives, God?! You know I have bills to pay. I'm a single mom, and I need a job. Why are you doing this?

All of a sudden, I heard a voice. Now I'm not talking booming pipes like James Earl Jones, but a kind male voice whispering in my ear that said, *"You got too comfortable there. We had to do this. You have work to do."*

Excuse me?

At first, I literally looked around to see if someone was standing behind me. That's how clear this voice was in my head. All I saw were a couple of homeless guys scratching themselves.

Now I'm hearing VOICES?

I'd heard about this kind of stuff happening, like when my friend Lisa Dietlin was hit by the cab. I just didn't think it would ever happen to ME.

Within minutes, the rumor mill had spread through the building that I had been let go, and my phone was blowing up.

"How is this possible? If this can happen to you, it can happen to anyone!" one coworker wrote.

"Say it isn't so!" another texted.

Rather than go back into "The Toxic Tower," I called a good friend and went for a three-hour lunch.

What are they gonna do, FIRE ME?!

By the time I got back to the building, it was time to meet Caroline. As I was sitting on a bench in the lobby, my phone rang. It was the woman who had hired me five years earlier.

"Did you go to the press?!" she screamed when I picked up the call.

"I haven't even told my family about this," I said, shocked at her tone. "Why?"

"Feder has an article," she said. If anything was happening in the world of media, Robert Feder had the scoop. "How would he know if you didn't tell him?"

"Well, I walked into an office with a smile, thinking I was finally getting promoted, and I came out looking like I had been kicked in the gut," I said. "It doesn't take an award-winning reporter to figure that one out."

"I'm sure you'll land on your feet," she said in the most callous tone imaginable.

"Gee, thanks," I said. "This place should be hiring ten more people LIKE me, not getting *rid* of me!"

I hung up the phone and felt the eyes of every person walking in and out of the building staring at me.

Is that in my imagination?

At five minutes to four, Caroline walked through the door, looking like a million bucks.

"How are you doing, sweetie?" she said.

"I'll be fine," I said.

I checked Caroline in with security and got her guest pass. As we walked to the elevator, I heard a song in my head. Since I was a child, I've found God talks to me in song lyrics. If I'm in a bad mood, I hear a tune about being happy. If I'm in a good relationship, a love song creeps into my brain. As I rode the elevator up with Caroline to tour the *Chicago Tribune*, I heard a steady drumming, followed by the inspiring lyrics to Steppenwolf's "Hold Your Head Up" . . .

How appropriate.

We got off the elevator and bumped square into one of my close colleagues.

"Jen, is it true?" she said, holding my shoulders.

"Yes," I said with a smile. "But I'll still be here for the next few weeks, tying up loose ends."

We turned the corner, and I looked back at Caroline.

"You are one very strong woman," she said, nodding her head with approval.

I took Caroline through the newsroom, which is like walking through Grand Central Station. Several people were not only shocked to see me, but amazed that I was touring someone through the building with a grin.

"And here is the page-one conference room," I said to Caroline, walking her inside.

Once again, the lyrics kept pounding in my head like a mantra.

Hold you head high, Jen.

I glanced behind me and heard one man say to the person next to him, "She must not have seen the Feder column."

✠ ✠ ✠

We walked out of the building and made our way to the restaurant. As we ordered our drinks, Caroline got down to business.

"I'm going to tell you a little story," she said, putting her napkin in her lap. "When I was in graduate school, I met a woman who had an incredible impact on me. Her name was Jane Trahey. She told me the story of her own beginning. She had been let go from a company in Texas where she got her start, and she decided as she walked out the door of the company that she could either be devastated or make a very bold decision. She had two hundred bucks, so she took a hundred of it and bought a damn good outfit. She took the other hundred and bought a ticket to New York and got on a plane, knowing she could stay with a friend. When she got to New York, she marched into the office of Estée Lauder and said, 'I can take your company to the next level. That's how good I am.' She just hit the **bold** button. She wrote the *New York Times* best seller *Jane Trahey on Women and Power*. It was out when we met. She was dressed to the nines, and Estée Lauder had no idea she was living on rice and beans. And she told me, 'They hired my spirit.' Sure enough, the company skyrocketed because of her. She was one of their major backbone players."

They hired her spirit.

"That's an incredible story," I said.

I then told Caroline about hearing a voice when I was looking at the river.

"It said, 'You got too comfortable there. We had to do this. You have work to do,'" I said. "I heard it plain as day. So apparently my sacred contract is *not* with the *Chicago Tribune*."

"It served a purpose," Caroline said, taking a sip of coffee and looking me straight in the eye. "Now, you need to invest in *yourself*."

Time to find that bold button.

A couple of months later, Caroline was my guest for my live interview series at the Wilmette Theatre, "Conversations with Weigel."

"How are you doing?" Caroline asked when she got to the theater.

"Well, I'm moving, selling my house, and reactivating my production company," I said. "I'm putting myself out there like never before. I'm doing more book talks and keynotes. So far, so good."

"When so many changes happen at once, Heaven is orchestrating the movements," Caroline said.

Heaven is orchestrating the movements . . .

We made our way on stage, sat in our chairs, and started the conversation for a full house.

"So take me back to how this all started for you," I said. "You're a journalist and editor, minding your own business, when you get this epiphany in 1983 that you can look at someone and understand why they are sick. Did you ever doubt your choice to 'come out' as a medical intuitive?"

"My entire life is the story of doing something that I never knew existed," she said. "And it's a tremendous blessing to have that because I never anticipated what my life could be. So when you ask, 'Did you doubt this choice?' there was never a choice. I didn't pick a career like I was going to be an artist. Here's what God did with me—the divine gave me no ambition to be something I have a genius for, which is medical intuition."

"You knew at a very young age that you were wired differently," I said.

"My sensory system, from the time I could sense, was always on 'high,'" she said. "My mother is here, and she will tell you when I was a kid and we would be driving down the street I would do readings on the houses. I would say, 'That's what this one looks like and that one and that one.'"

"So you could see inside?" I asked.

"It wasn't seeing, it was like my radar was like a bat," she said. "I simply got impressions, one after another after another. It was my normal way. And I'm so grateful to my mom and my dad, but especially my mom, because she helped me feel safe with my intuition. As I started teaching classes all over the world, I've encountered so many people who say, 'I thought I was so weird or strange because I heard things or saw things or had psychic senses.' Whereas in MY case, I was so safe in my intuitive skin, and I still am. I look at people who didn't have that, and I think, 'How is it even possible for you to leave your house being so unsure of what's in the invisible world? How can you function so filled with doubt?' I never had that. Ever. I told my mother when

I was seven, 'In this life, I will be a writer.' When I was nine, I said, 'I will never marry.' I saw this clear as a bell."

"So for those who don't have the radar that you have, what do you recommend they do on a daily basis to try to tap into their true calling and their intuition?" I asked.

"You don't have to do anything to develop intuition, but you do have to work to develop your own sense of self-respect and integrity and your own sense of self," she said. "The question is why do you NOT listen to yourself? Why do you NOT trust that gut instinct within you? Because your gut instinct is always engaging within you. Your conscience is a high voltage part of your intuition. 'Is this right or is this wrong?' Do you actually need to stop and do a whole big meditation when you know that you're lying? You better not. Your whole sense of self-esteem is based on whether or not you are negotiating your self-worth. The more you know that you are betraying yourself, your whole inner self says, 'What are you doing?' and you lose respect for yourself.

"In all my years as a medical intuitive and evaluating illness and why people become ill and don't heal—and I've done over 12,000 readings in my career and have worked a long time with physicians and the whole nine yards—one of the reasons most people cannot bear to be attuned to their intuition is their pathological fear of being humiliated. And because people fear being humiliated so much, however they've constructed their idea of God, they think there is this off-planet man that wants to punish them, which is such nonsense."

"And you were raised Roman Catholic and admit to loving many things about being Catholic," I said.

"Yes, so I get to say this," she said. "This is a mythology that there is an off-planet God, and if you're really close to God, God will take your money and make you suffer. And it's like we play this really coy game with spirituality where you want to pray, but not that much. The other reason people do this is because they want to retain their relationship with darkness because it's convenient and it works. People do not trust light; they trust darkness. They want to make sure they can still lie and do things in the dark. Whereas if you decide to really tune in to your intuition, really fast, you have to own it. 'I heard that. I'm clear.' When you stay in the darkness, you can say 'I'm not sure,' and then you do whatever you want. People do not like the light, there's no buzz in it. It's not erotic. Darkness is erotic. There's a buzz. What we have is a fear of the light, just like you have a fear of being fully healthy."

"Why would people fear being healthy?" I asked.

"The fear is that once you're healthy you cannot be vulnerable," she said. "Once you're healthy, you cannot go into your excuses. You can never ask for help. You can be asked for help, but you cannot be vulnerable. Once you're fully healthy, then any kind of fragility is not allowed. That capacity to need someone is going to go away."

"You mentioned recently that this is a really important time to be alive," I said. "Can you explain?"

"My opinion is that we are living at the most extraordinary time in the history of civilization, and that is a big huge sentence," she said.

I'll say!

"That may be the biggest sentence that ever comes out of my mouth, those words that I just used," she continued. "It is a real privilege to be alive now. You can't go through the days of your life now with your eyes closed. This is a privileged time in history. It's also a very tumultuous time because it is so privileged. They go hand in hand. And you cannot afford to *not* be aware of what is happening to the best of your ability. We are entering a galactic community, and it's time to stop acting and promoting the mythology that we exist alone in this Universe. The former secretary of defense in Canada has been continually releasing videos in which he is openly admitting that Canadians have been in touch with four different groups of extraterrestrials. Pope Francis, this present pope, initiated a council of theologians, astrophysicists, astrobiologists, philosophers, and they are constructing the first galactic theology. Why? Because they know we're in touch with extraterrestrial civilizations, at least four of them, and they know that all world religion mythologies are crumbling now. We are living through this because they are all Earth-centric—they all promote the idea of an Earth-centric God. Every major war has revolved around what people believe in the scripture. And it's barbaric. The divine doesn't have a religion. It has a cosmos. It has galaxies. I'm not taking away Christmas, you can still have Christmas, but if any of what you believe tells you, 'You are different than me and I must close the door in your face,' then you are not a follower of what you believe. Christ was all about love. Every single holy being has taught love. That's it. They didn't teach to kill because someone believed something else. And we are living at the end of those mythologies. So the next level of myth has got to be created."

"A lot of what you write about is that by serving, you heal. In community you heal, and by serving you actually thrive," I said. "It's not just about writing the check, it's about dealing in and getting off the couch. Dealing in is really important to healing, isn't it?"

"Absolutely," she said. "If I was your angel preparing you to descend into life and I had to say, 'Okay, there are certain things that are going to happen to all of you, so it would be in your best interests to not take your own life personally, and if you start thinking that these things are only going to happen to you, that's when you get yourself into trouble.' People think they should be the exception. The moment you think you're exceptional, the moment you want to *be* exceptional, and the moment you *believe* that you were born to be exceptional is the day you sign up for suffering."

"Is that because you can never meet your own expectations or because then you are disconnecting from source and community?" I asked.

"You're disconnecting from your own nature," she said. "You are looking to be the exception, and the reason we've become such a lawless society and soulless, because we are both, is because most people believe their purpose in life is to be exceptional. So we have a society in which people have contempt for the ordinary. They name their kids Sunshine Meditation Karma. They tell you their kids are 'special.' They haven't done anything! Why are they special?"

"But you as a child, doing readings on the houses with your mom, that's pretty *special*," I said.

"But my mom didn't tell me that, I earned it once I was an adult," she said. "We are creating a group of narcissistic, dysfunctional human beings, and their survival mechanisms are not engaged because there's no reason for them to have to survive because they're all wrapped up in helmets and washcloths. Before they came along, people survived the planet without Handi Wipes and helmets. And they did just fine. We've got to get over ourselves, right? Have you had enough of yourselves yet?"

"You don't think there are some kids who have gifts that others don't?" I asked.

"Sure, look at Mozart," she said. "There have always been brilliant children. But what we are doing now with calling our children 'special' is nonsense."

"How much illness do you think is because of absorbing other people's energy?" I asked.

"Everyone in this room, you think of yourself as having five senses, but in fact you should think of yourself as having ten senses," she said. "You actually should be thinking of yourself as a hologram. If I walked up to you and popped myself behind you and you didn't hear me, you would jolt because you could feel my energy coming right into yours. So start thinking of yourself as living in this whole field, that's number one; and number two, you are accustomed to thinking in terms of time, that this way was yesterday and that way is tomorrow. You have a sense of history and future when in fact everything is in the present. Time is a made-up thing."

"Do you believe in past lives?" I asked.

"It's not that there is a physical version of you somewhere else, but it's energetic," she said. "Let's say that I die. We're all going to die. The part of me that goes on, let's say I've reincarnated to 2050. The part of me that lived now, and the part of me that lived in WWII or in Elizabethan England, those parts are still active in my psyche. To the best of my ability to understand it, those parts of me are still influencing and speaking to me. They are active agents. They are not dead. It's no different in a way than an event that happened in your childhood still speaks to you and influences who you are today. It is a participant in how you feel and in your health, relationships, vocabulary, in everything."

"You came to the show I did with Manhattan Medium Thomas John," I said. "Do you believe some people have the gift of mediumship or psychic abilities?"

"Yes, it's rare," she said. "And Thomas is totally authentic. And believe you me, I am such a miserable critic because I've seen so many frauds. They are carnival barkers. He is the real McCoy. I have so much regard for this young man. We had a breakfast privately, so I said, 'Why do you do this? If you didn't have something to say to them when they were alive, shame on you,' and he said, 'Because I think it could be useful.' So when you were interviewing him on the stage, he had such a solid presence.

"So Thomas and I are walking home from breakfast, and he said, 'Who is Mary Pat?' That was my brother's wife. Then he said 'Ang and Alison?' Those are his daughters. She goes by 'Ang.' So he's scoring points with me. Since then, we have had some exchanges about very significant messages, and I didn't feed him any information at all."

"So you see how his gift helps with grief," I said.

"Yes," she said. "And people have a hard time healing when they are holding on to grief. Grief can block healing energy very easily."

Grief can block healing energy.

"But I also think you have to be so careful about who you ask and why," she said. "There was a very famous psychic, and she was not real. She did a lot of harm. There was that kidnapping—Elizabeth Smart—and she said that she was dead, and of course she wasn't. And I have a friend whose husband disappeared off of a yacht, and this psychic said he was dead and it turned out he wasn't. You have to trust your gut. When you go to someone who isn't real, you put yourself at risk for hearing something you can't get out of your head that could be very damaging to you. Don't go to someone for questions that are based on fear. If you are fear-driven, you will find someone operating at the same temperature as you."

"I think one of the most powerful stories in your books is about David, the Native American who was a prisoner in WWII," I said. "Will you tell that story?"

"You guys want to hear an incredible story?" Caroline asked the crowd.

"Yes!" the room answered.

"I'm privileged to say David Chethlahe Paladin is the one who told me this story," she said. "He was a Navajo, and he left the reservation when he was about thirteen years old. He was an alcoholic, and when he left the reservation, he lied about his age and joined the Marines. And he went to war. He was a code talker and was captured by the Nazis. They brutally tortured him—nailed his feet to the floor. He eventually makes it back to the US and lived in a VA hospital, but his legs were useless so he had crutches.

"He returned to the reservation, and they hadn't seen him since he was thirteen and a half years old. His intention was to see his people and say goodbye to them before going back to the hospital. In his tradition, they have a healing circle in which they listen to you tell your story three times. They want you to empty yourself three times—so your body, mind, and spirit can tell the story. They won't listen to it a fourth time because at that point they think they are then serving you to keep the story *in* you. They feel the story has your spirit captured and then you get sick every time you tell the story.

"So David told the story three times, and they felt that it didn't heal him. So they took his crutches, and they put a rope around his waist and threw him into the cold water. And they said, 'Either you call your spirit back or we'll stand here and watch you drown.' He said that's exactly what they did. He was in the water struggling, and as he prayed for his spirit, he saw the men he hated so much for what they did to him. He had to forgive them and actually let go of the resentment and hatred he had for them for what they had done. He saw that they were doing their part in the war. Remember when I told you not to take things personally in life? What they did to him wasn't personal—it was the hatred and madness of war. Though it hurt him personally, the war wasn't created just to torture him. In his ability to see this, he forgave the men, and he got his legs back. He became a Navajo medicine man and a painter, and he became a Christian minister. He was a remarkable man. That is the power of forgiveness."

Caroline then took some questions from the crowd. She addressed everything from lactose intolerance to breast cancer. And then there was one woman who worked as a healer and felt her illness "came out of left field" and wondered why she didn't know she would be getting ill because she had a good sense of intuition.

"I feel like I should see it coming," she said.

"Okay, the idea that you can see an illness coming, let's drop that," Caroline said. "Nobody says when they get sick, 'I've been expecting you!' Are we done with that? We think illness and health should follow logic, and it does not. 'There must be a reason for why this happened to me,' or 'if I could find THE LESSON, then it will all go away.' Oh, really?"

"But you do say some pains in certain parts of our body can be caused by emotional things," I said.

"But there is logic to the energetic anatomy," she said. "That's not the same as creating a God mythology that is saying, 'You gave me this illness for a reason. If I could find the reason, then you'll get my life back the way it was,' right?"

"So for her to be the best healer, she should get herself in alignment?" I asked.

"No. Stop," she said, pinning my ears back. "Don't think, 'If I do this, then this.' Enough."

Caroline directed her attention back to the woman who asked the question and looked her right in the eyes.

"You don't feel malignant to me and I always can pick that up," she said. "You don't have cancer. You don't have a blood disease. I'm scanning you. This is the thing that keeps coming up, 'If I'm doing everything right, then illness shouldn't happen to me.' That's a bogus model. It just doesn't work that way. 'If I'm a good little girl, God won't punish me.' And that's not the way the universe is ordered. In the way the universe is structured, illness is not a negative. It is in *our* world. It's not to the universe. It just IS. So if you look at it like, 'This is just something that I'm going through, for whatever reason,' it would be much better. It's got nothing to do with right or wrong, good or bad, 'What is the lesson?' 'Why is this happening to me?' That's for children. Now you're just dealing with the flow of creation. Ask to understand the flow of life within you. Say, 'My body is finding difficulty with this flowing.' That's what tai chi is about: the flow. It's not about solving problems from the 'right or wrong' paradigm anymore. 'I just want to balance the flow of my energy.' What makes a master is that eventually you don't have sides. You have flow.

"I've seen people heal in an instant. I had a workshop where a woman had arthritis so bad, and then in the workshop, her hands opened up and were healed and she was terrified to leave the room because she was afraid her hands would go back to the way they were. But she was fine. And that was when I was starting to introduce prayer into my workshops, which I hadn't done in twenty-five years, but I saw more and more spontaneous healings happen again and again. People can heal at the speed of light. And what prevents people from healing at the speed of light is that it's too fast for them. They can't adjust the rest of their lives to having been healed that fast. They can't hold the power of the miracle in them. They can't contain the miracle."

They can't contain the miracle.

"At the same time I think someone can go to bed healthy and wake up fully cancerous because the reverse is equally true," she said. "You can't have the sun without the moon."

"You talk about having a very prayerful life," I said. "Before we go, would you share with us one of your prayers?"

"I will always be astounded by the power of prayer—to me, prayers are answered the moment you say them," she said. "I'm going to give all of you some nuggets of wisdom to take home."

Yahoo! Wisdom "to go"!

"At the end of the day, your greatest companionship is to know truly that your life matters in ways that logic will never be able to help you with," she said. "And worrying about the future is one of the biggest wastes of time in your life. You keep your attention in your present. And when it comes to your health, you say, 'I'm doing everything I can, and I know with *you* all things are possible.' There's no such thing as a terminal illness, just as there's no such thing as terminal health. Say, 'This is my experience for today. This is the body you want for me today, but I could wake up tomorrow and my body could be totally healed.'

"And when you go to sleep, do what I do. I call the angels in, and I say, 'Take me out of my body and repair it while I sleep. Take me with you someplace, repair my soul in the night, and repair my body while I sleep.' And let the graces pour into you. And one of the most wonderful prayers of Teresa of Ávila is, 'Hover over me, God. Keep me still and keep me in grace.' That's all. You don't need more than that."

That night when I got home, I heard the sound of my ten-year-old son's cold trailing down the hallway. I went and got some honey out of the kitchen to give him a spoonful for his cough.

"How was your show?" he asked, making a face as he swallowed the honey.

"It was good," I said. "Why don't you lie down, and I'll rub your feet."

"Great," Britt said, lying on his back and sticking his foot in my face, which was our nightly routine.

"So my friend Caroline has a prayer she says before bedtime that I'm going to say for you now," I said, rubbing the arch of his right foot. "I think it might help your cold."

"Okay," he said, now fully relaxed.

"She says we need to call in our angels, and then say, 'Take me out of my body and repair it while I sleep.'" I said.

"Dear angels, please take me out of my body and repair it while I sleep," he said.

"And then say, 'Hover over me, God. Keep me still and keep me in grace,'" I said.

"Hover over me, God," he said, his eyes half open. "Keep me still and . . . and then do what?"

"Keep me in grace."

"What does that mean?" he asked.

"I guess it means to keep you in a peaceful loving place," I said.

"Okay. Keep me in grace," he said.

"Good," I said, reaching for his other foot.

"Great-Grandma Virginia wants you to know she loves what you did to the earrings," he said, his voice getting softer.

"Huh?" I said, confused. My Granny Virginia died when I was fifteen.

"The earrings you're wearing," he said.

After Virginia died, I inherited a pair of her earrings. She didn't have pierced ears, so I had taken them to a jeweler to have them updated. For the first time in years, I had put them on that night before heading to the theater.

"When did she tell you that, honey?" I asked.

"Right now. She's right there," he said, pointing to the ceiling with sleepy eyes.

Paging Thomas John, Concetta Bertoldi, and Rebecca Rosen!

I thought about the words of Caroline from earlier that evening.

"I'm so grateful to my mom and my dad, but especially my mom, because she helped me feel safe with my intuition."

"Well that's great, honey," I said, trying to be as supportive as possible. "Tell her I love her so much."

"She knows," he said. "She loves you, too."

I looked up at the ceiling and smiled.

"Good night, sweetie," I said.

"Good night, Mom," he said. "I love you."

"Love you, too," I said, placing my hands on my earrings.

That night as I was dozing off to sleep, I decided to give
Caroline's prayer a try. And then I added a list of things I'm
grateful for to up my game:

*Dear God, universe, guides, and angel-posse. I'd like to
thank you for helping me remember that you're up there. I'm
so glad that Caroline told me you're not waiting to punish me
and take my money. Since love and forgiveness seem to be the
keys to healing, I'm going to do my best to spread both, even to
the assholes who cut me off in traffic. Thanks to Concetta for
teaching me that even though my dead relatives can see me
in the shower, they aren't passing judgment on my attempts
to sing show tunes. Thanks to Paul for the reminder that
fear and love cannot coexist. That one really stuck. (Maybe
I'll print up some t-shirts?) I'm also going to give my worries
"to the altar" as Paul suggested, although it may be more of
a shelf, since "altar" sounds really churchy to me. Thanks
to Rebecca, Thomas, and Concetta for being so willing to
talk to dead people. I have seen your messages work miracles.
Thank you Echo and Judith for showing me what it's like to
"walk your talk" in the intuition game and for empowering*

me to trust that my intuition is actually working. Thank you to Michael for helping me not only get past my fear of ghosts, but for being a kindred spirit by saying "fuck" whenever the mood strikes. And thank you so very much for the teachings of Caroline, who encouraged me to invest in myself when nobody else would and to not take anything in this world personally because . . . (wait for it) it's not about ME. What happens in this world is not "good," and it's not "bad." It just IS. (That one is really hard for a journalist, by the way, but I'm working on it!) Thank you for allowing me to help people heal through my words instead of having me shivering on an overpass in the pouring rain saying "Traffic sucks. Back to you in the studio." I'm glad we both finally figured out that my sacred contract is to tell inspiring stories.

Oh, and thank you for my incredible son, Britt, who taught me what it means to feel unconditional love. While Caroline may not agree, I KNOW that kid is "special"!

If all goes as planned, I'll see you tomorrow,

Love,

Jen

ACKNOWLEDGMENTS

THANK YOU—

To all the mediums, psychics, and healers who agreed to let me use their wisdom in this book! In alphabetical order, that would be Concetta Bertoldi, Echo Bodine, Michael Bodine, Nikki Bodine, Thomas John, Caroline Myss, Judith Orloff, Rebecca Rosen, and Paul Selig.

To the friends who joined me on this adventure (you know who you are), thank you for being willing to be vulnerable in front of complete strangers who said they were talking to your dead people and x-raying your soul. Dinner is on me.

To my son, Britt, for making me want to be a better person and reminding me what it means to feel unconditional love.

To my family, for supporting my desires to tell stories that some people (well, I guess *most* people) think are strange.

And finally, thanks Greg Brandenburgh and the folks at Hampton Roads/Red Wheel Weiser for believing in me and for publishing my work.

Until the next adventure!

Stay spiritual, dammit!
—Jen

ABOUT THE AUTHOR

JENNIFFER WEIGEL is an Emmy Award-winning journalist, Chicago television personality, author, and performer who owns her own Chicago-area production company. She lives in Evanston, Illinois. Visit Jenniffer online at *www.jenweigel.com*.

HAMPTON ROADS PUBLISHING COMPANY
. . . for the evolving human spirit

Hampton Roads Publishing Company publishes books on a variety of subjects, including spirituality, health, and other related topics.

For a copy of our latest trade catalog, call (978) 465-0504 or visit our distributor's website at *www.redwheelweiser.com*. You can also sign up for our newsletter and special offers by going to *www.redwheelweiser.com/newsletter/*.